THE PSYCHIC SECRETS OF A

By: JONATHAN ROYLE – (c) 2015

www.MAGICALGURU.com

THE PSYCHIC SECRETS OF ALEX-LEROY

By: Jonathan Royle (c) 2015.

Welcome to this Short Publication within which you will discover the exact techniques that I used back in the early 1990's in England to regularly become featured and declared as a "Genuine Psychic and Clairvoyant Spiritualist Medium" in such publications as The Psychic News Newspaper amongst many others.

In the very early 90's I worked extensively in the Northwest of England and also Yorkshire Areas as an apparently genuine Psychic, Clairvoyant and Physical Medium, under my then stage name of Alex-Leroy.

As well as giving Tarot, Palmistry, Numerology and Astrology Readings on a one to one basis for House Parties and also at Psychic Fairs, I would on regular occasions perform with other Mediums within their Theatre and Civic Hall "Evening of Clairvoyance" demonstrations and then after having done a few of these I gained a manager.

That manager whose "Stage Name" in the Spiritualist and Psychic World was Nathan Demdyke, but whose real name was and is Peter Keefe, had in the past worked for Doris Stokes touring "Contacting the Dead" shows and he took me under his wing.

Consequently my own one man "Bridges from Beyond" (An Evening of Clairvoyance, Spiritual Healing & Physical Medium-Ship) demonstrations was put together and these always drew large audience's and ultimately big profits for all concerned.

By Early 1995, partly because my Stage Hypnosis Career path had taken off so much and was keeping me so busy, and partly because I had developed a conscience, I decided it was time to cut my ties with the Spirit World.

And so I wrote a series of articles explaining the methods I used for the Magic Magazine published by Geoff Maltby of Repro Magic Company in London, namely Club 71 which later changed its name to The Magician.

These articles I wrote were heavily edited down before publication, as space was limited in the magazine, and so within the pages here, I intend to firstly share with you the five articles exactly as they appeared in editions of Club 71 Magazine during 1996 and 1997.

And then I want to share with you the bits that were edited out and finally I will go on to expand upon these writings and reveal to you even more of the closely guarded Secrets and Techniques that are used by many if not all of the Worlds Most Famous and Successful Spiritualist Mediums and Psychics.

I know that what I am about to share is the real deal as I actually went out there and extensively performed in the real world as a Genuine Medium, Clairvoyant and Psychic.

I was featured numerous times as "the real deal" within the pages of

International Publication "Psychic News" which at the time was a print newspaper, but in more recent years has become a glossy magazine.

I have met in person, spent time with, discussed and shared secrets with and even worked alongside some of the big names of the Psychic Industry as it was in the 90's and as a result some of the revelations within these pages may seem either too outlandish, too simple or too obvious, but I can assure you they have all been used in the real world to great effect.

Which Reminds me, when you get a chance do a google search on "Psychic John Sutton" and then do a search for "John Sutton Derek Ackorah" and another one for "John Sutton James Byrne" and finally one for "John Sutton Wayne Isaacs" and when you do, I predict that you will find it odd that this John Sutton character is named as the author and/or co-writer of various of these peoples books on how they are Psychic.

Seems they all needed a Ghost Writer, excuse the pun!

However I can tell you that John Sutton not only Ghost Writes many "Psychics" books including those where his name is kept secret, but also he, just like all the other Psychics I have ever worked with is a complete con artist and uses Cold Reading galore in his work.

I appeared on British TV Show "Funky Bunker" with him on ITV back in 1996 when I was doing Psychic Belly Button Reading and he was telling me about all sorts of scams he had pulled and techniques he had taught James Byrne and other so called Psychics to use in their work.

Speaking of James Byrne who once filled the London Palladium with his "Contacting the Dead Show" he himself has actually admitted that it is all just a massive scam and much can be learnt from his comments here:

http://www.skeptic.org.uk/magazine/articles/120-from-psychic-to-sceptic

Indeed they are all still being used in the real world in Spiritualist Churches and in Hotel Function Rooms, Civic Halls, Theatres and other venues where big money can be made helping people to apparently make contact with and get messages from dearly departed loved ones who have now passed over to the Spirit World.

So Let us begin our short journey and please remember I did all of this in the real world and put it all into print in one form or another **BEFORE** any of the people such as Luke Jermay, Paul Voodini, Jerome Finley, or indeed any of the other recently established "names" in Mentalism released their works on the Questions and Answers Act (Q and A) as Magician's and Mentalists Like to call it.

I was using these techniques as far back as 1989, and first put many of them into print in 1995 (when I sent them to Club 71 for consideration) so that is around 26 years since I first used them in action whilst doing one to one readings and/or Public Platform demonstrations of Mediumship and is around 20+ years since I first put pen to paper about these methods.

Indeed here is a quote from Former Editior of the International Brotherhood of Magicians "The Budget" Magazine, Jack Griggs which appeared in **"The Order of the Magi"** magazine back in 2011.

"He began by giving information of his beginning in show business, at the age of 3 as a Clown assisting his father in a touring Circus. He wasn't happy with this and turned to Magic with the aid of library books. He later at the ripe old age of 14 turned to Mentalism & Cold Readings. This was when I first met him, as having got my address he called at my house. I saw him performing and was surprised at his ability in this field. I can attest to his claim to have made a lot of money at it. However he gave this up as he was uncomfortable with people believing that he was a genuine Psychic and went back into Magic and Hypnotism."
Jack Griggs – Order of the Magi Magazine 2011

NOTE: The features Editor of Club 71 was Walt Lees and Executive Editor Geoff Maltby, I mention this as sometimes Editors notes were added to my articles, but one of most interesting is the fact that they confirmed in writing that they had seen numerous of the feature articles that "Psychic News" and other Publications had published about me within which I was declared as being the "real deal" and stated to be a 100% Genuine Spiritualist Medium.

Anyway it is now time to Let the Fun Begin...

THE PSYCHIC SECRETS of Alex-LeRoy

Part 1: (Originally Appeared in Christmas 1996 Club 71)

Bridges from Beyond.

I intend to get straight to the point and teach you the inside secrets that I learned from some top professional mediums and psychics.

If you doubt my credentials, I can furnish ample proof that, using this knowledge, I was able to convince Psychic News and other "experts" that I was indeed "the new Uri Geller and Doris Stokes rolled into one".

(Editor's comment: I have personally seen some of Alex's many press cuttings and can therefore verify this claim.)

Should you be sufficiently unscrupulous, following my instructions will enable you to become known as a walk-on-water psychic.

Alternatively, you may prefer the more honourable course of using this knowledge to debunk those, who make vast fortunes from such spurious claims.

The first and main requirement, to put any of these techniques into operation, is a combination of astuteness and unmitigated gall.

You must also be able to think on your feet, keep your wits about you, improvise to take advantage of anything that happens, observe as much as you can and have a good basic understanding of human nature.

It is rather like being a salesman, barrister, diplomat or politician.

Another important point is that you must not, in any way, appear to have the least knowledge of conjuring methods.

So it goes without saying that none of the items used in your demonstration should be anything commonly associated with sleight of hand or illusion.

Also, avoid using props that will not stand up to strict examination.

Some of your work will be under so-called test conditions, where sceptical people will feel free to challenge and restrict you.

If you think all this is limiting, bear in mind that you are not required to produce any spectacular effects.

Doing so could be counter productive.

Your audiences will be mostly people, who want to believe in your powers.

They are looking only for small signs, not earth-shattering miracles.

BUILDING BRIDGES

Perhaps the best way to proceed is to outline the workings of my own one-man show, which I called Bridges from Beyond.

I will take you through it, step by step, exactly as I did it, explaining the details as we go along.

Imagine the audience are assembled and the first half, lasting approximately forty-five minutes, is about to begin.

Very important, at these events, is setting the right atmosphere.

The choice of background music can go a long way towards this.

While your own musical tastes may not be the same as mine, the recordings I used proved most effective.

The overture music is Do You Believe in Miracles? from the soundtrack of the film Leap of Faith which stars Comedian Steve Martin and itself is a great training aid in the "Psychology of the Psychic".

Then comes a recorded voice-over introduction - Ladies and gentlemen, please welcome live on stage, for an evening you will never forget, Britain's Fastest Spiritualist Medium, the "new Uri Geller", the one and only, the amazing Alex-LeRoy!

My play on music, as I enter and make my way to the microphone, is the Unchained Melody which you may recognise as being the theme tune from the film Ghost.

This sets the desired atmosphere instantly.

The presentation then starts in low-key manner.

At these events, you do not have to fight for the audience's attention or really do much to win them over.

Their own (some would say misguided) faith has brought them.

They are eager to hear messages from their departed loved ones.

So do not be afraid to keep them in suspense.

A long, opening speech will be patiently listened too and accepted.

Thank you very much indeed ladies and gentlemen for that over whelming reception.

Welcome to what's going to be, for most of you I'm sure, a truly interesting, informative and entertaining hour or two.

Now the reason I say "most of you" is that many of you will be receiving some form of communication from a loved one in spirit, or, hopefully, receiving some healing by the power of psychic energy.

Now although tonight is mainly a serious demonstration of both verbal and physical medium-ship, I would prefer it if we all had the occasional laugh along the way, because no doubt there's likely to be a few tears, too!

For those of you who have never seen a professional medium in action, I'd just like to point out that there is no need to be afraid at any time.

The reason I say this is because it's not unusual, in these types of demonstrations, for people to receive a message from a spirit, themselves, or to feel one walk past them or, maybe, even to find that the hands on their watch have moved on several hours, or even your keys may have bent out of shape.

It matters not what happens. These are just signals from loved ones in spirit and as such you have nothing to fear.

(The above all serves to plant suggestions in the minds of the more susceptible. It ensures that, afterwards, some people will convince themselves that they have experienced these things.)

Now the other main thing I need to point out is that I'm not a miracle worker. I'm just a medium, well at least that's what it says on my underpants!

Seriously, as a medium I act rather like a satellite dish, transmitting messages from loved ones in spirit to you, here in this world.

Just like a satellite system for a TV set, the reception can sometimes be a little unclear or mixed up.

So please bear with me when I am trying to communicate a message to you.

A simple "Yes" or "No" after each piece of information will suffice.

(This covers you for any mistakes you might make, or general inaccuracies.)

Well, that's just about all the serious stuff out of the way.

But may I relate to you a short story about a late, great medium Mr Harry Rare?

Mr Harry Rare was one of the first spiritualist mediums. By day he was a circus midget at Blackpool Tower Circus and by night he gave demonstrations of clairvoyance, at a time when all this sort of stuff was viewed as witchcraft and was illegal.

Indeed, I remember reading that one night at a demonstration, the Blackpool police showed up and tried to arrest Mr Rare.

Luckily for Mr Rare, the police were unable to catch him as he was so small that he ran off between their legs.

The next day there was an amusing headline in the Blackpool paper which just said "Small Medium at Large".

Another time, a few years later, when Clairvoyance had just been legalized, Mr Harry Rare was called in by the Blackpool police to use his powers of psychometry to try and help find a very young boy, who had gone missing, while his family were on holiday.

Mr Rare was given a coat, which the boy had worn and after concentrating he said, "For sure, this boy is safe and he's in Nottingham!"

He then went on to give the police a name and address at which the boy would be found, The police visited and, believe it or not, the boy was at that address.

Apparently, he had met a girl while on holiday in Blackpool They had fallen in love and when the girl had returned to Nottingham, the young boy had run away in order to be with her.

Thanks to our hero, medium Harry Rare, the family were reunited and the Blackpool newspaper carried a huge story with a humorous headline that went "Well Done, Medium Rare!"

Anyway, ladies and gentlemen, enough about the past.

Only the other day I was in a supermarket when I saw another psychic, who said, "You're OK Alex! How am I?"

And if that wasn't funny enough, the other night I played poker with a pack of Tarot cards. I got a full house and the person next to me died.

Finally, ladies and gentlemen, I'd just like to say that although I've only got crystal balls - it may be a disability - but I shall be doing my best tonight to get some form of message from the spirit world for each of you.

But first I'd like to carry out an experiment to see how receptive all of us in the room are to one another...

Now comes an item called the Psychic Third Eye Projects the Answer. I will tell you all about that in the next issue.

THE PSYCHIC SECRET'S of ALEX LE-ROY

Some readers may recall that I described this in the now defunct and lamented Magigram several years ago.

At that time. I did not explain it within the context of the show, so I make no apologies for offering a rewritten version, here.

Part 2: (Originally Appeared in Spring 1997 Club 71)

The Psychic Third Eye

Last time. I began to describe my Bridges from Beyond show and had just covered the lengthy introduction.

Having set the scene. I would commence the first demonstration, which I titled the Psychic Third Eye Projects the Answer.

As you will be frequently reminded during this series, psychics are not in the business of performing clever tricks.

So most of the chicanery tends to be pretty basic stuff and the effects low-key.

People are looking for small signs of greater powers, not spectacular illusions.

In fact, if the magical element is too strong it will be counter productive.

A few simple mysteries can have an impact on the minds of convinced believers that is out of all proportion to what they would with a normally sceptical audience.

Such is the case with this item.

I will start by describing the method.

Cards are featured, which may appear to contradict my earlier warning about never employing props commonly associated with sleight of hand.

However, cards are different.

Fortune tellers and psychics do use them extensively.

So they can be brought into a show like this without arousing suspicion.

But they must not be handled in a manner suggestive of any adeptness or dexterity.

REQUIREMENTS AND PREPARATION

Five new packs are needed, all with different back designs.

Carefully remove them from their cases without breaking any seals.

After they have been stacked. you are going to replace them in their original boxes, so that they appear untouched.

With most brands, you can work any cellophane wrappings open at the bottom and slide the cards out that way. but as different manufacturers tend to adopt particular methods of packaging, you are really very much on your own for this part.

So far. 1 have never failed to find something suitable in my local stationers.

Each pack is then arranged in the Eight Kings sequence, i.e., 8, king, 3, 10, 2, 7, 9, 5, Queen, 4, Ace, 6, Jack, repeated four times with the extra joker placed at the face.

For this effect, the suits can be in any order as they play no part.

So one of the system's great weaknesses is automatically eliminated. The other joker(s) is/are inserted anywhere in each pack.

The packs are next returned to their boxes, which are resealed. gluing if necessary.

Although you should complete the job as neatly as possible, nobody gets much of a look at the result, so it does not have to be able to stand up to close scrutiny.

Just in case anyone does not already know how to mentally remember the order of the cards, this is done by using a mnemonic that goes:

Eight kings threatened to save ninety-five ladies for one sick knave

Each word of this little nonsense rhyme keys the value of a card,

i.e.. Eight (8) kings (K) threa(3)ten(10)ed to(2) saveC) nine(9)tyfive(5) ladies(Q) for(4) one (A) sick(6) knave (J)

Just remember that seven is "save" and six is "sick".

All this may seem like a lot of preparation but only one pack will be broken open at each performance. So when it has been done, you have only to prepare a single replacement for every subsequent demonstration.

METHOD

Now for the crude mechanics of the trick, after which I will detail the patter and presentation - the really important part.

Five packs are brought on and an audience member asked to pick just one.

As all are stacked in the same way, this makes no difference to anything, but to the lay mind a free choice seems psychologically fairer.

After all, who would imagine anyone taking the trouble to prepare five packs and then not use four of them?

Remove the chosen pack from its case, which is then thrown carelessly to the floor.

This suggests that not only did they have a free choice of pack but, due to the seal, there is no way you could have tampered with it.

Be careful not to even mention that the case is sealed.

Simply break it open without comment.

People will see what you are doing and the fact that you appear to attach no importance to the wrapping is further evidence of its genuineness.

On big shows 1 would have a stooge, who pretended to work at the theatre, bring on the packs.

Otherwise I would ask a member of the staff to help by keeping hold of them (in a paper bag) until required.

Because of the patter, the audience will be misled into thinking that this person has actually purchased the cards.

The chosen pack having been unwrapped, it is then handed to another spectator - nominated by the person who chose it - so as to give an air of freedom and no possible force.

This new spectator is asked to fan the cards towards themselves and remove the Jokers.

The fact they handle the pack and look through it also psychologically suggests it is unprepared.

With the random suit order. nobody will notice the cyclical set up.

You then take back the cards and do a couple of false shuffles nothing fancy - which leave them undisturbed.

The pack is then handed back to the person, who is asked to cut it a few times.

The audience will remember afterwards that the cards were shuffled and cut but will forget who really did what.

As we magicians know, completed cuts do not disturb a cyclical set up.

The assistant is then asked to give out ten cards to ten different people in the audience, who must hold them against their chests so no one can see what they are.

While this happens, turn your back to strengthen the impression of test conditions.

You must verbally suggest that she gives them out in a straight line order from left to right.

That way you will know when you turn around who has which card.

The remainder of the peck is then returned to you and you place it into your pocket.

As you do so. glimpse and remember the bottom card.

From this you will be able to calculate what the top one would have been had it not been removed, eg if the bottom card was a King, the top one would have been a three - the next one in the mnemonic order.

This is the card value that the first person will have. Name it and then just carry on in the order of the set up for the other nine.

PATTER OUTLINE

For the experiment I'm about to attempt I'll require your help.

Without that the test is doomed. We all have what is known as a third eye.

This is, if you like, the psychic eye and it is located at the centre of your forehead, just above your nose .

Later, I'll be asking some of you to project your thoughts with this third eye.

Don't be scared when you try, it can not harm you but you may feel a slight tingling sensation in your body as you do it and some of you may see a bright blue light coming forth from other people's heads.

This is what is called an Aura and again there is nothing to be afraid of!

(Because you have suggested these things might happen, some people will actually experience them or at least, say that they have!)

"A couple of weeks ago I telephoned the theatre and asked if they could get one of their staff to purchase five different packs of cards and bring them along tonight That way we can be sure no one has got to them. So could that member of staff bring them up. Please"

(The stooge brings up the bag with the cards.)

"I shall ask you three questions and I want you to answer honestly and clearly Have we met before? Did you buy these cards yourself? Has anyone at any time been able to tamper with them? "

(Of course she answers "No!" to the first question. "Yes!" to the second and "No" to the last, due to the fact that she is lying through her teeth. If you are using a genuine member of the staff, eliminate the second question.)

The person will interpret the remaining two to mean "Have we met before tonight!" and "Has anyone at any time been able to tamper with them, since I gave them too you?"

(The audience, of course, will put a different slant on the answers.)

"Okay, thank you Can I have the bag now please"

(Take the bag. remove the packs and get a spectator to select one. making it obvious they have had a free choice. Next the first spectator picks another assistant, who does everything as stated earlier until you end up with ten people holding one card each.)

"You now have one card each - those ten of you that were picked at random by the person who was picked at random by the first person.

I would like the people with cards to now look at them and remember what number or letter their card is.

Forget about the suit as that would make the test harder than it already is under these conditions

"I want you to remember that number, or if you have a Jack, think of a big 'J', for Queen a big Q and for King a big K '.

Can you make your mind blank except for your giant number or letter, whichever the case may be.

Now please see the letter or number glowing in a bright blue light and try to project it through your third eye at the centre of your forehead.

(You now turn around and face them.)

Close your eyes, concentrate on the number or letter and project it with your third eye so it glows like a bright blue neon shop sign.

As I said, some of the more psychic ones among you may be able to see these signs and those transmitting them to me may feel a slight tingling sensation in their bodies as they do so.

But this will go as soon as you stop transmitting...

Well done, the room is lighting up with bright blue letters and numbers
You are all certainly very receptive to these special powers.

I shall now tell you the numbers and letters I am seeing for each of you
and. when I do if it's right please hold the card up and shout 'Yes. correct! '

The audience will then give you a round of applause for helping.

If however, as so often happens with these tests, I get your card wrong,
hold the card up and shout 'Wrong' You will still get a round of applause
from the audience for doing your best

Wow for the first card I can see this clearly It is the number ten (or
whatever)

(The person does as requested and the audience applaud. This is repeated
for card two. For card three you appear to struggle)

"This light is not so clear. I'll come back to it at the end

(Cards four. five and six are guessed correctly)

and then you purposely get card seven wrong.

Cards eight, nine and ten are then named,

Finally you go back to the third person.

Ask them to make their mind go blank and visualize a television set in
their mind's eye.

Onto this they must then project the letter or number.

You act as if finding it hard to pick this up and then say a letter or number
as the case may be.

They shout out ""Correct!' and. believe me. if you have built up the drama and tension enough. you will get a tremendous ovation.

Say they can keep the cards and should they find special markings on them as some sceptics have suggested in the past, then you will write them a cheque for a thousand pounds.

THE PSYCHIC SECRETS of Alex Le-Roy

Part 3 – (Originally Appeared in Easter 1997 Club 71)

After the previous demonstration come the first of the Clairvoyant messages that will be periodically given to individual audience members.

These, not the magic, are what bring people to the performances and what the show is mostly about.

Mainly, they are just convincing rubbish, which is capable of different interpretations and nebulous enough to be applicable to almost anyone.

They can be interspersed with bizarre statements of pure gobbledegook such as:

"I see you have a blue aura, which tells me the spirits are offering healing to you and all will be well!"

or

"I've just seen an older gentleman spirit place a rose on your lap madam. I'm told it will mean a lot to a member of your family."

Once, during the evening. I would throw in a scandalous message to an anonymous spectator, e.g.,

"I won't say who the next message is for to save them embarrassment but you'll know who you are and I hope it helps you in your quest to find life's answers."

Occasionally, you can make use of a stooge or two.

To them, you give in-depth messages.

If you get the chance, try to attend a few performances by stage mediums and also go to a few different Spiritualist Church Services and see several different Mediums in action and you will see just how easy it really is.

Note the ambiguous phrases that get bandied around and the cop outs.

For instance, a good line I once heard when a person claimed not to understand the message they had been handed went,

"Take it with you and ask your family members. They will reveal just how relevant it is!"

So as you see, being a medium is a no-lose situation.

If you sound confident and authoritative, keep your wits about you and use your observation, the gullible will fall for it.

OPEN MIND

After the messages, this next item was supposed to demonstrate my powers of thought transference, mind reading etc.

It just used a thumb writer to complete a prediction once I knew what I was supposed to have foreseen.

In my routine, I predicted three things: how much loose change somebody had in their pocket; the last four digits of a serial number on a banknote; the initials of an audience member's relative who was now deceased and living in the spirit world.

The whole thing was presented quickly, taking not much more than a few minutes to complete.

The method is too well-known to require any elaboration here.

If you really do not know what I am talking about, Geoff will be more than happy to sell you the necessary gimmick for a modest price.

The previous demonstration was immediately followed by more clairvoyant messages to audience members, then came:

THE LEVITATION TEST

This very old stunt is still unknown to a lot of people.

So much so that even Uri Geller makes occasional use of it.

You will need a chair and the assistance of five members of the audience.

One person is seated and the other four each interlock their fingers, with the forefingers "steepled".

Two of them then put their projecting forefingers under the seated persons armpits.

Two others put theirs under his/her knees.

All are then told to attempt to lift the assistant on the count of three.

Mostly they will be unable to do so. or even if they do mange, it will only be with much struggling and heaving.

Explain that with a little psychic energy, they can all become ten times stronger and will be able to lift the person easily.

All four are instructed to place their hands on the seated person's head.

Say that this time when you count to three, they will have been filled with psychic energy and are to resume their previous positions.

They do so and once again you give the signal. This time, they do lift the person easily.

Quite how or why it works I am not sure but I bet that it is due to natural, physical causes and owes nothing whatever to the supernatural.

However, the effect is staggering.

After this demonstration, four of the people returned to their seats, while the fifth was kept behind for:

CRAZY TIME

This is fully explained in Ben Harris's book Gellerism Revealed The basic effect is that a spectator's watch is removed and placed face down in their closed fist.

After concentrating, the spectator opens his or her fingers to discover that the watch hands have been psychically moved by several hours.

To get all the working details you will need to buy the book.

The Ben Harris handling is not mine to disclose.

However, the basic principle is not a new one, so I can tell you that. It is simply that, when you first take the watch from the person, you quietly pull out the winder.

Then as you turn the watch face down and place it on their palm, your thumb secretly flicks the winder a few times causing the hands to move.

In closing his fingers around the watch, the spectator actually pushes the winder back in.

The important thing is not to look at your hands as you do the dirty work and to keep talking.

The rest is down to pure presentation and suggestion. Take your time and repeatedly ask if they can feel the watch getting warmer as you concentrate.

They will, because their own body heat warms it up.

Imagination does the rest.

At the finish the assistant went back and I would announce an interval.

I then exited the stage to more strains of Do You Believe in Miracles? and the curtains closed.

THE PSYCHIC SECRETS of Alex Le-Roy

Part 4: The Second Half

(Originally Appeared in Summer 1997 Club 71)

I seemed to get spirited away from the last issue (Sorry, my mistake! - Ed.) but now I am back to tell you about the second half of my show Bridges front Beyond which lasts about an hour.

Again the play on is Do You Believe in Miracles? followed by a voice over:

"Ladies and gentlemen, please welcome back, live on stage, Britain's Fastest Medium, Alex-LeRoy "

As with the introduction to the first half, the opening patter may seem a little long winded to magicians. They instinctively want to get on with the tricks, but this is not a conjuring show and I am not supposed to be an illusionist.

Thank you once again ladies and gentlemen for that truly overwhelming reception. Now as you have probably guessed already, almost anything can happen during a demonstration such as this.

In fact, to be honest, these things surprise me as much as they do you.

With clairvoyance and psychic medium ship results are never guaranteed So please bear with me in this, the second half, where I intend to demonstrate that there is life after death.

Firstly, though, I'd like to tell you a brief story about one of the greatest mediums of all times, the late, great Doris Stokes.

I well remember that my uncle once visited her for a reading and asked her what the spirits were able to tell him about sport - and was their any sport in the after life?

Doris made contact and said yes, indeed, there was some sport in the next world, to which my uncle asked. Are there any football teams?

Once again. Doris consulted the spirits and after a short pause she said, Well I've got some good news and some bad news.

The good news is that yes, indeed, they do have football teams.

My uncle was reassured He then asked what the bad news was.

To which Doris replied. 'Well the bad news is that you're playing in goal next Tuesday!

Seriously, though, before I start, I'd like to warn you all never to play with Ouija boards - and I mean never.

Playing with a Ouija board is like leaving your front door open and letting anyone you don't know come in.

You have absolutely no idea which spirits are evil or good and you never know when or indeed if you'll be able to get rid of them again, So please don't mess about with them.

Now comes Colour Projection, which is presented as a test to see how receptive the audience are to the performer and vice versa.

The full handling can be found in Let the Audience Do the Show by George Anderson.

You will need to refer to that book for all the details, but here is a short description to give you the basic idea.

It works because of natural psychology based on the colours most people are likely to think of and the order in which they will do so.

Required are six cards, roughly jumbo size. Their backs are plain but the faces are different colours.

One is red, another blue, then come yellow, green, white and black - in that order.

Red is the colour that most people will name first, if asked to call one out. Black is likely to be their last choice.

White usually comes second to last.

Hold the cards in a fan. so that the faces are towards yourself.

The audience, who cannot see the colours, have to try and read your mind and guess which one you pull out of the fan first.

Remove the red one and ask, "Who is thinking of red?" A lot of hands will shoot up.

Show its face, with a smile and congratulate those audience members who successfully named it.

Put it down and repeat the experiment by removing the Blue. After Red, most people will think of Blue, so the majority will again get it right.

Then pull out the Yellow, followed by the Green and the White, in that order.

Many of people will guess them all correctly.

Those who do feel good about themselves, suspecting that they might also have latent psychic powers.

So really, there is no magic or trickery.

It is just a straightforward demonstration of a simple psychological principle, but because of the situation, it takes on a totally undeserved significance.

People want to believe, so they do believe.

At the finish, a few more clairvoyant messages are given out to various folk. These messages, as has already been mentioned, are the main attraction for most of the audience.

The hope of contacting a deceased loved one is the thing that draws them to the show. The techniques to use have already been discussed in earlier articles and there is nothing to add at this stage.

In the next issue, I will detail how the performance continues.

THE PSYCHIC SECRETS of Alex-Leroy

Part 5: Conclusion

(Originally Appeared in Autumn 1997 Club 71)

This part will take us right up to the end of my one-man show Bridges from Beyond.

In the last issue, I outlined the opening of the second half.

From there I would move to the Psychometry test.

Here you borrow a finger ring and have the lender tape it to the inside of a paper cup.

This cup is then mixed up with five identical cups, while your back is turned.

One by one. using mind power alone, you eliminate each of the empty cups, leaving only the one containing the ring.

The secret is ludicrously simple.

You would wonder how it could fool anyone but, in this context you are not supposed to be a magician, so the audience are not looking for trickery.

They are getting plenty - but they are not looking for it!

The cup you casually hand out, for the person to tape the ring inside, is marked with a light pencil dot on top or perhaps even just a fingernail nick in the edge of it.

The rest is pure acting.

Having returned the ring, a few more messages are given out, then comes a simple One-Ahead routine, involving three people, who seek healing.

It is done as a sort of preliminary test to precede the obligatory psychic healing part of the show.

Most magicians are familiar with the principle. You write something on a card and place it down. A person is next asked a question and the audience told to remember their answer.

You then take up a second card and repeat the process with another spectator, after which, you do likewise with a third.

The three cards are now displayed and it is seen that you correctly predicted each person's answer.

The method is simplicity itself and most readers will already know it.

You need three blank cards, anything between playing card and postcard size will do.

Take up the first, look at somebody and then draw a triangle inside a circle.

Put the card down, without showing the design and ask the person where they would most like to go on holiday.

Suppose the reply is Paris, remember this answer and look knowingly at your prediction.

Now pick up a second card and gaze at someone else.

After a few moments, write the word Paris and place the card down.

Then enquire of the person, "What's the first flower that comes into your head?'" Many people will think of a rose, but whatever the answer, remember it and go to the third person.

Take your last card and, as you gaze thoughtfully at this participant, write the word Rose or whatever flower was stated.

Address this person, "Forgetting a square, which is too obvious, name any two geometrical shapes and imagine that one shape is inside the other."

Most people will say circle and triangle. If not, they will probably name one or the other, together with something else.

Octagons and tetrahedrons do not spring quite as readily to many minds.

Even if the person insists on a cross inside a hexagon, two of your predictions Paris and Rose will still be correct.

However in truth the vast majority of the time they will say Circle and Triangle.

You drew a Triangle inside of a Circle and can ask them if this is what they imagined , most often they will say yes.

However if they say they imagined the Circle inside of a Triangle, you can respond:

"Argh that makes sense, I did feel a little confused as to what I was picking up, but I did keep getting the phrase, A Circle and Inside a Triangle"

"I thought it meant the Triangle was inside the circle but obviously they were telling me to draw a Circle and that it should be inside a Triangle" In the "Spiritualist" and "Genuine Psychic" setting this makes things seem even more impressive to them.

These are only experiments remember, and with the type of audience that come to these demonstrations, even if you only got one of them half right it would be sufficient evidence of your powers for most of them.

Now comes a spiritual healing sequence and a mass audience healing test.

For this kind of thing, there are two basic secrets - the power of suggestion and a couple of stooges.

Do not use too many of the latter just the odd one or two.

Mind over matter will, can and does do wonders.

You will be amazed how many people will profess themselves healed - and may even be so, by the power of auto suggestion.

(**Editor's comment:** This kind of pseudo healing can be dangerous Suggestible people, believing themselves cured, may ignore their doctors ' advice and suffer a worsening of their condition. So you could find yourself responsible for a death. We do not recommend that you use "healing" other than in the context of an exposure.)

After healing a few people by the laying on of hands, I would ask the entire audience to join hands with myself forming part of the chain.

I would say that this allowed my psychic energy to pass from person to person, seeking out those who needed it most.

Stacks of people would claim afterwards that attending a performance made them feel better.

After the healing came the Fastest Medium demonstration.

This is a development of the usual Clairvoyant messages that were handed out during the earlier parts of the show.

But the technique was to give short messages to as many people as possible in rapid succession, as though trying to get around the entire audience.

Very soon, everyone would lose track of where I had reached and become unsure of who the message was intended for.

Consequently, they would just have latched onto anything that sounded appropriate to themselves.

Remember that the sort of people who attend these performances all believe in this kind of mumbo jumbo and want to receive messages.

That is why they have come.

The Metal Bending routine that followed and with which I used to finish, is dependent on the Key Bending gimmick sold by Taurus Magic (Derek Lever) and the usual spoon bending techniques.

By now, most magicians know that a spoon can be weakened by flexing it repeatedly backwards and forwards until it is almost on the point of snapping.

It can then be returned to its normal shape until needed.

A slight shake or gentle stroking will cause it to bend visibly or even break in two.

A few such spoons can be quickly prepared and picked out of a box of un-gimmicked ones.

After a few minutes of this sort of thing, much of it improvised. I would say a quick goodnight and exit to the strains of the Unchained Melody, which is allowed to play almost to the end. as it is a tear jerking number

Series ends.

EDITOR'S POSTSCRIPT

During the readership survey last year, a number of people complained about this series, saving that they found it offensive.

The idea of setting oneself up as a fraudulent medium, in order to cynically extract cash from gullible and sometimes desperate people is a far cry from magic as entertainment.

However, that sort of thing does go on.

Unscrupulous people are out there doing it and magicians have a useful role to fulfil in the debunking of such charlatans.

To do so effectively, they need to know the methods used and why they work.

Alex has done all would-be debunkers a favour by discovering and revealing how seemingly normal people are taken in by this sort of hokum.

In publishing his findings, he has rendered magic a great service.

<u>BEYOND THE CLUB 71 REVELATIONS</u>

Perhaps the most important thing to remember is that although as Human Beings we generally would like to think of ourselves as unique, special and individual, the **REAL TRUTH** is that basically speaking we are all essentially the same!

We all Piss and Shit the same, and we all have the same basic desires, needs and wants, the same general motivations and aims in life.

This is something that becomes very clear when you read the book **"Passages"** which was originally released by **Gail Sheehy** back in 1976.

Just as I was advised to by those who taught me these Secrets fast approaching three decades ago now, I too would unreservedly recommend that you get hold of a copy of **"Passages" by Gail Sheehy** and study it very closely indeed.

You would also be wise to take a look at another of her books called **"New Passages"** and subititled **"Mapping Your Life Across Time"** which was released in 1996.

Both of these books will help you to be able to read people from "Cradle to Grave" just by getting an idea of how old the person you are speaking to is and what sex they are (male or female) and hey presto what you have studied in these two books will give you more than enough to give very detailed and extremely accurate readings about what is going on in that persons life, what feelings and emotions they are truly having in their life and a whole bunch of other stuff that people will perceive that you could not possibly know unless you were truly Psychic and/or getting messages from the other side.

Also in this regard I would suggest that a read of an article that I wrote for the World's Biggest Personal Development website "Self-Growth" will help to make things a little clearer.

The article is online at:

http://www.selfgrowth.com/articles/the-keys-to-hypnotic-success-how-to-be-truly-happy-healthy-content-in-all-areas-of-your-lif

However the text of that article is reproduced below:

THE KEY'S TO HYPNOTIC SUCCESS

By: Dr. Jonathan Royle – **www.magicalguru.com**

As is well known within the Psychotherapy world "We are all products of our environment" or to be more accurate:

"We are all products of our environment, unless we are given the tools and opportunities to positively expand beyond the confines of our direct environment"

You see to function Positively, Happily and Harmoniously in life (on all levels) we need to as human beings (especially as we are growing up) to feel:

Loved – Wanted – Needed – Appreciated – Cared For – Cherished and Valued

If there is a lacking of or disruption in any of those 7 Positive Pillars then it will most likely lead to that individual suffering a negative impact on their:

Self-Confidence, Self-Esteem, Self-Image and/or Self-Control (Willpower)

And sadly when there is a disruption or negative impact on one or more of those 4 vitally important Foundations of "Self-Worth" then this can and often does regretfully lead to the individual feeling…

Negativity, Trapped, Worthless, Like A Failure, Angry, Resentful, Frightened,

And even more depressing is the very real fact that when one or more of those 7 Negative Pillars is in place that it can often lead in one or more ways to the individual going into

SELF-DESTRUCT MODE

And that combined with negative environmental factors can be the straw that breaks the camels back so to speak and can lead to a downward spiral which could include things as extreme as them turning to a life of:

Crime, Self-Harming, Drugs, Alcoholism, Domestic Violence, Prostitution, Homelessness or even worse in extreme cases Suicide…

These are most always destructive behaviours and actions that manifest themselves either as an extreme reaction to or negative result of the Emotional impact of what has been going on in and/or lacking in their life's.

Often for example Youngsters can get involved with a "bad crowd" as this gives them a sense of belonging and despite the negative consequences of such "gang culture" can help to fulfil the gaps they may feel inwardly in those 7 Positive Pillars and those 4 vitally important Foundations of "Self-Worth" which I mentioned earlier.

And once the downward spiral starts it can and often does lead to a lifetime of destruction which negatively impacts not just the individual, but also their family, friends and even often many members of the community as a whole (in the instances of crime etc.)

HOWEVER THERE IS A WAY WE CAN HELP STOP THIS HAPPENING

But the great news is that when an individual is helped to discover ways to expand their horizons, try new things, gain a sense of achievement, given a chance to grow as a person and starts to realize that there are better options available for them and that a brighter future is a possibility for them then this can work wonders in helping them to positively impact and develop their:

Self-Confidence, Self-Esteem, Self-Image and/or Self-Control (Willpower)

And when they grow in these areas, the 4 vitally important Foundations of "Self-Worth" they can then start to feel a sense of:

Positivity, Personal Freedom, Positive Self-Worth, Success, Courage, Achievement, Happiness.

And perhaps not surprisingly as a positive side effect of these beneficial changes they will finally be able to learn to **LOVE THEMSELVES** and of course gain **SELF-RESPECT**

This can lead to a whole new perspective and positive approach to life, can help the individual to gain a whole new positive support and positive social network and so ultimately can also lead them in the long term to a more Positive Environment and thus consequently help them to gain the 7 Positive Pillars in their life's of positively feeling:

Loved – Wanted – Needed – Appreciated – Cared For – Cherished and Valued

Now fortunately for the majority of people, a lacking in one or more of the Positive Pillars does not usually lead to such negative results as the few examples given earlier, however it is my experience that this is always without doubt or exception the Ultimate under lying reason and cause that people develop Bad Habits, Addictions and other personally Negative and also Self Destructive Behaviours.

A lack or imbalance in one or more of the Seven Positive Pillars will always in some way lead to some kind of less than beneficial behaviour and/or thought patterns and thus it is true to say that a lacking or imbalance in one of these area's starts to lead the person away from Pleasure and sets them on the road towards Pain.

Therefore it is also true to note that doing therapeutic work in order to enable the lacking or imbalances in those areas to be eliminated so that the person feels fully 100% Positive and Complete in the areas of:

Self-Confidence, Self-Esteem, Self-Image and/or Self-Control (Willpower)

Will then ultimately mean that any previous lacking or imbalances in the following Seven Positive Pillars will set themselves right and thus enable the person to be the Perfect Them:

Loved – Wanted – Needed – Appreciated – Cared For – Cherished and Valued

It is with this model that I created (as outlined above) that I formulated my creation of "Complete Mind Therapy" and is exactly what the "Non Specific Treatment Script" which is included in my book "The Encyclopedia of Hypnotherapy, Stage Hypnosis & Complete Mind Therapy" by Jonathan Royle which is available from all major online book retailers deals with so effectively.

In a nutshell it is my belief and experience, based on my almost 26 years working as a Professional Hypnotherapy Practitioner at time of writing this (Jan 2015) that when you consider the above and put things right in those areas that everything else will fall positively and permanently into place for your clients.

If you think deeply about this, you will, I am sure also realise that offering a person the chance to be the centre of attention and creating an On Stage environment where they feel:

Loved – Wanted – Needed – Appreciated – Cared For – Cherished and Valued

Is also the True Key Motivating Secret of how and why a Successful Stage Hypnosis show works and when you bear this in mind I am sure your shows will become more successful, just as your results with therapy sessions will also.

To fully understand this further consider that one end of the scale is Pain (lacking or imbalances in these areas) and the other end of the scale is Pleasure (balance and completeness in these areas) and then consider when reading about "Pain and Pleasure" therapy in my book (mentioned earlier) in the section about Complete Mind Therapy how this can be used to so easily help the client to make changes in their life in a manner that proves far more successful than you may ever have thought possible.

Consider that the negative end of this scale can also be called "Out of Control" and the positive end termed "Self-Control" and perhaps things become even clearer for you?

And then consider that the negative end can be termed as "Trapped" and the Positive end as "Freedom"

Or indeed it could be "Unhappy or Depressed" at the Negative End and HAPPY & JOYFUL at the positive end.

Or perhaps you'd like to consider that one end of the scale is Stressed/Anxious and/or Tense, whereas the other end of the scale is Relaxed, Calm and Positive.

In all cases however the route from one end of the scale to the other is through and by dealing with the personal attributes and feelings that I have repeated several times during this short article.

And now I have to say that without doubt to understand this fully and the sheer possibilities of what I have just taught you, right now you would be wise to go to your local book store and order a copy of the excellent book Psycho-Cybernetics, A New Way to Get More Living Out of Life by Maxwell Maltz.

Also consider that in life **FAILURE** occurs because of:

F – rustration

A – ggressiveness

I – nsecurity

L – oneliness

U – ncertainty

R – esentment

E –mptiness

And as you should by now realise all of those things relate back to what I have discussed already. Then at the other end of the scale **SUCCESS** in life occurs due to the following:

S – ense of direction

U – nderstanding

C – ourage

C - almness

E – steem

S – elf – Confidence

S – elf – Acceptance

Again I am sure you can see how that all relates back to the Positive Pillars I mentioned before.

Read Psycho-Cybernetics, A New Way to Get More Living Out of Life by Maxwell Maltz and consider it in light of what I have discussed in this article and I feel certain that on all levels you will become a far better Psychological Mind Therapy Practitioner.

The following are Six Further Books that I also consider vitally important to your success in Hypnosis and would say that you should read as soon as possible:

1) They Call It Hypnosis by Robert A. Baker.

2) If This Be Magic – The Forgotten Power of Hypnosis by Guy Lyon

Playfair.

3) Monsters & Magical Sticks – There's No Such Thing As Hypnosis by Steven Heller.

4) Bad Medicine: Misconceptions and Misuses Revealed, from Distance Healing to Vitamin O (Wiley Bad Science Series) by Christopher Wanjek.

5) Trick or Treatment: The Undeniable Facts about Alternative Medicine by Edzard Ernst & Simon Singh.

6) Influence: The Psychology of Persuasion (Collins Business Essentials) by Robert B. Cialdini.

And of course it goes without saying that I would recommend you take a closer look at my "Encyclopedia of Hypnotherapy, NLP and Complete Mind Therapy" series of books that are available from all major book retailers.

Our time together for this short article is almost at an end, but before we part company allow me to just draw your attention back to the Key Pillars that we mentioned earlier of:

Loved – Wanted – Needed – Appreciated – Cared For – Cherished and Valued

If there is a lacking of or disruption in any of those 7 Positive Pillars then it will most likely lead to that individual suffering a negative impact on their:

Self-Confidence, Self-Esteem, Self-Image and/or Self-Control (Willpower)

At this point I suggest you get a dictionary and closely examine the meaning of all the words that are in bold text, as then you will start to fully realise that although at first site they seem like very similar emotional states and/or feelings, in actual fact they are all very different indeed.

Perhaps one of the most important points to remember is that these are all Emotions and that means Energy in Motion, which is E-Motion.

All Emotions have a feeling connected to them for Human beings and that feeling moves in a certain direction.

If that direction is the wrong one, then the feelings the person will be experiencing will be negative and our job is to help them change the direction of those feelings so that the e-motion (energy in motion) starts to move in the opposite and therefore positive direction.

In other words we take them from where they are now to the opposite end of the scale, we help them to Change Things To The Opposite...

And that is why so often Talking Therapies and Psychological Mind Treatments and Therapy approaches are referred to as "Change Work"

Ultimately however the individual must be ready for change to take place.

In my opinion and experience based on all I have seen and done with clients over the past almost 26 years, they all already have the solution to all of their problems within them, its just that either they don't realise that, or more often than not, they have come to realise that but are now scared to make the changes for themselves.

You see when (if they have) they come to realise that all they need is within them, they will also on an unconscious level at least realise that they could now make those changes they desire for themselves and indeed will also come to realise deep down that they always could of done.

In other words they come to realise that they only have themselves to blame for not having made the changes sooner, but this realisation is in itself painful as to admit such to them selves and others who may say "why did you not do it sooner?" would make them feel silly and perhaps also guilty for not having done so sooner.

However if they have to come to see a therapist such as us, then they can use their treatment and time spent with us as their reason and excuse for now being able to make those changes.

That means that all blame is removed from them for not having been able to make the changes for themselves sooner on their own.

It means they can leave behind any guilt that could have played on their mind about not having made the changes sooner, as the treatment with us the therapist proves that they could not do it on their own, although as we both know in truth they actually could have done so!

Therefore it is my experience that any drawn out, Ritualistic Process, to which a sense of importance is attached and which is delivered by the therapist to the client in a manner that displays and transmits the intent that this always work and will work for them, will ultimately become so believable for the client that it can be their Focus and Catalyst for change.

The Ritualistic Process is the Trigger Point that sets off the Placebo Process and also gives them Permission to change and also an excuse and reason to change in a manner whereby they can feel good about themselves and not have to dwell on the very real fact that they could have made those changes sooner if they'd really wanted too.

This I have found is made even easier if you get them to imagine images of change occurring and the more bizarre, comical and/or ridiculous and abstract these images are the more positive impact they will have, as my experience confirms that the unconscious/subconscious mind reacts most rapidly to outrageous images and symbolism.

As the saying goes "What the Mind of Man Can Perceive and Believe, It can Achieve" and indeed that is very much the case with the Client and Therapist scenario.

We merely provide an environment whereby they can Believe that change is possible and create the expectation that the ritual we carry out with them will work and as a result the changes can and will take place.

For now my final thought for you to ponder is the very real fact that Emile Coue who coined the phrase "Every Day in Every Way I am Getting Better and Better" discovered that if we repeat such positive affirmations (suggestions) to ourselves at least 3 times in a row on three occasions each day so that it becomes an important ritual and also includes the repetition factor that helps things to bypass the Critical Faculty and thus ultimately enter the unconscious directly then extremely positive and permanent life changing results can and will occur.

This illustrates not only the power of ritual and repetition, but also highlights how important Suggestions of a positive nature are in our work.

Our time together is now at an end but you may wish to participate in a "Virtual" online treatment video session that I have put together at **http://www.magicalguru.com/therapy-sessions/** as this session is designed to specifically deal with all the emotional pillars.

I'm sure you'll both enjoy it and also find it very beneficial, indeed I'd love to hear your thoughts and feedback on this article and the virtual online session and can be contacted on **royle@magicalguru.com**

(c) 2015 - Dr. Jonathan Royle
Creator of Complete Mind Therapy (CMT)
Creator Of Mind Emotion Liberation Techniques (MELT)
Clinical Hypnotherapy & Psychotherapy Practitioner

Incidentally the points mentioned in that article also apply to How and Why Spiritual Healing works **(when it does)** and anybody considering doing anything connected to Spiritual Healing would be wise to read all of the books that I recommend in that article.

The truth is they will give you a far greater understanding of people and make it far easier for you to give them accurate readings and/or messages from the other side.

Something else that it would truly behove you to do a little study of is **"Maslows Hierarchy of Needs"** and in that regard a good read of the information at this web page is sincerely advised: **http://www.simplypsychology.org/maslow.html**

And these two videos are well worth a watch, the first outlines "Maslows Hierarchy of Needs" at **https://youtu.be/EH04OsNuvcw** and then in this second video you will learn about the Expanded Hierarchy of needs **https://youtu.be/yM8SwZkvCIY**

When you've studied those books and watched those videos I have no doubt that you will finally truly realise and understand the very real fact that we are all basically the same.

Next you need to master the Art of Cold Reading and in that regard there is truly only one book you need to study and that is **"The Full Facts Book of Cold Reading: A Comprehensive Guide to the Most Persuasive Psychological Technique in the World"** by Ian Rowland.

I wish that Ian's book had been around when I started doing readings and Clairvoyance shows as it would have saved me an absolute ton of money.

In short everything of worth, that I ever learnt from every other book on the subject that was available back in late 80's to early 90's is pretty much contained within the pages of Ian's excellent publication.

I would however also suggest that you get a copy of my Ebook **"Cold Reading for Magician's and Mentalists"** which is available from https://sellfy.com/p/oon4/

From that particular publication I am reproducing an extract here below which will not only whet your appetite but also will expand upon what you have already learnt in this book.

Cold Reading For Magicians & Mentalists

(The Lazy Man's Guide to Tarot, Astrology, Palmistry & Psychic Style Fortune Telling)

(An Extract from the 127 paged A4 Book)

Welcome to "Tarot Reading for Magicians & Mentalists", I truly hope you find the techniques taught within as useful and powerful with your clients in the real world as I have done for the past over 25+ years of using them with more people than I care to remember.

As my time and space is short, I'll get straight down to business and start by suggesting that you listen to the audio recording of a Radio Interview I did years ago on Psychic World Radio within which I explain my Rapid Tarot Mastery System.

The Recording which is **One Hour & 17 Minutes** long also teaches my proven variation on the NLP Fast Phobia Cure and can be heard at this Private **(so please don't share)** link at: **http://youtu.be/3K320aYebkg**

Incidentally although similar in content to what the late and great Joe Riding explained in his book "Learn the Tarot in Seven Days" this is actually in truth based on the contents of several much older books, and by much older I mean decades older including one I have sat here entitled

"The Tarot Made Easy" which was printed **circa 1960** and which I purchased many years ago for less than $5 in an old Occult Book store inside the Corn Exchange in Manchester City Centre (England)

Anyhow starting from the simple memory system explained in the audio recording, your next step is to sit down with your deck of Rider Waite Tarot and to one at a time pick the cards up and do exactly as follows:

01) Pick up A Tarot Card and Stare at it for a Minute or Two, being sure to look all around the card and pay attention to all the images in both the foreground of the picture and also those in the distance as well.

02) Then close your eyes and take a few nice deep breathes in through your nose and then out through your mouth before you take in breathe number four which you can, this time hold for a few seconds and then let it out rapidly like a giant sigh as you notice how this helps you to relax.

03) Then make an image in your minds eye of the Image on the Tarot Card that you were just staring at a few moments before, make it as clear as possible inside your mind and then imagine being able to climb inside the image on the card and entering into the picture.

4) Next as you enter the picture in your minds eye take a few minutes to explore what you can see including all that is off the card, yes that's right in your minds eye imagine being able to walk off the edges/sides of the Tarot Card image you saw before and being able to see and explore what else is there.

05) After a few minutes of this, allow the image to fade away as if drifting off into your mind, like a cloud being blown away into the distance by the wind and then open your eyes and look directly at the Tarot Card which you were staring at before.

06) Pick up this card and turn it face down onto the table in front of you and then start this 6 step process again with the next Tarot Card in the pack. This whole process should take no more than around 6 minutes for

each card, and of course you could choose to have breaks every now and again or spread the 78 card deck out over a few days. But in total at 6 minutes per card by 78 cards, that is only 468 minutes which is Seven Hours & 48 Minutes in total.

NOTE = However airy fairy the above 6 step process may sound, let me please assure you that setting aside a day of your time to go through this process with all 78 Tarot Cards after you've taken on board the simple memory system explained in the audio recording, will without doubt help you to give far more detailed, interesting, accurate and flowing readings.

And that leads us nicely to the next piece of the jigsaw which is **YOU MUST HAVE COMPLETE CONFIDENCE IN YOUR ABILITY** as a Psychic Reader in order to be able to be so relaxed during the giving of your readings, that you both learn to trust in your intuition **(yes I did just suggest you say the first thing that comes into your head and trust your gut instinct)** but also because you being relaxed will have the knock on effect of helping your clients to relax and in turn when they relax they will communicate with you more **(both Verbally and Non Verbally)** without them either realising it or remembering it after the event.

To this end I offer another resource to help you by way of this video and audio recording which will take you through a session of my unique Hypnotherapy Approach of Complete Mind Therapy and help you to programme your mind for complete confidence and total success as a Psychic Reader and Consultant.

Simply set aside **92 Minutes** when you won't be disturbed and then participate with the recording you will find at this Private Link (again please don't share as others pay for access to this special recording) **http://youtu.be/j5xsE4036uI**

The only important thing to remember is that whenever I talk about the Television Set, at this time think of an image of yourself when you knew nothing about Cold Reading, Tarot Reading or anything similar. A time when you were full of self doubt and lacked the confidence to be a truly successful Psychic Consultant.

And then whenever I mention the Magic Mirror, at those times be sure to imagine an image of yourself as "The Worlds Greatest Psychic Reader" and imagine yourself getting positive hit after positive hit each and every time you tell your clients things.

Do all of the above and then you'll be ready to go and start doing readings, the quality and accuracy of which, will I am sure amaze you as much as they do those you are reading for.

However it won't hurt to have a few more tools and techniques on your side and to that end here is the exact word for word script that I use at the start of my readings when people sit down at my table at Psychic Fairs or when they enter my office.

I'll explain the Psychology, Reasoning and Hidden Power behind it mostly as we go along, and then will clarify a few points at the end. However for now just imagine your name is Sharon and that you've just sat down at my table for a reading....

"Well Hello There And Good Day to you my lovely, my names Jonathan Royle"

(at which point I put my hand out to shake hers and then look her in the face and remain silent for a second or two at which point she will usually tell me what her name is and if she does I nod my head at her as she does, if however she does not tell me her name then after a couple of seconds I continue)

"And Your name is?"

(she responds in this example and says Sharon, and just as stated before I stare into her eyes and nod as she says her name and then I follow up with)

"Is that the name that you like your Close Family and Real Friends to Call You?"

(If yes that is fine, but more often than not it will be a nickname or shortened version of their name for example Shaz, that they now reply with at which point I continue and say)

"So would it be OK if I call you Shaz during the reading as it will help me to connect with your energies more easily?"

(99.9% of the time they will reply Yes that is fine, at which point they have just accepted you into the same Psychological circle of trust that they already place their closest family and most trusted friends into and so instantly their guard will be down and things become easy. However should they say no, this also is valuable as it tells you that its an awkward truly sceptical and untrusting person that you have in front of you and that itself will help guide the reading, but as I say 99.9% of the time I find they always say Yes its OK to call them by that name)

"OK That's Great Shaz, so Have you ever had your Tarot Cards Read before?"

(Allow her to answer and stay quiet until she stops talking, seriously often they will tell you everything you ever need to know to be able to feed back to them later in the reader in a disguised manner that your hard work is over at this point, but it all seems so innocent due to the nature of the question and it seeming a logical thing to ask. Anyhow she will either say Yes or No)

FOR NO = "Well Shaz, before we begin, I just want to let you know that if the Death Card Appears, it does not mean your going to fall off your chair and die, in actual fact it usually means the end of a chapter in some area of your life and the opening of a new door and opportunity for the future, OK?"

FOR YES = "That is great Shaz, in which case, I expect that you already know that if the Death Card Appears, it does not mean your going to fall off your chair and die, in actual fact it usually means the end of a chapter in some area of your life and the opening of a new door and opportunity for the future, OK?"

And then I continue:

"What I'd like you to do please Shaz, is to take the cards and give them a mix or a shuffle, or cut them a few times, basically just mix them around and mix them up so you know they are in a personal and unique order just for you to help us with our reading today"

(She Starts to Mix The cards)

"Oh and Shaz, if there is any particular issue or area of life that you'd particularly like to ask the Tarot about and gain insight to and answers about, then **PLEASE DON'T SAY IT OUT LOUD TO ME**, but rather just think about it as you mix the cards and let your energies flow into the cards"

(She will mix and think, but more often than not start telling you stuff here despite the fact you told her not to! When this happens, let her tell you the key points and then stop her boldly saying **PLEASE SHAZ I DON'T MEAN TO BE RUDE BUT DON'T TELL ME JUST MENTALLY ASK THE CARDS**. She will forget ever telling you these things by the end of the reading. If she does not say anything be sure to keep an eye on her lips more than I care to remember the people will speak to themselves as if whispering the question and you can often make it out, which they will never be aware of or remember. I then continue)

"Great Shaz, so in a moment I'd like you to take 13 cards out of the Tarot Deck from anywhere you feel drawn towards and then place them face down on top of each other in a pile here on the table"

(I point to spot on the table)

"As that way we know the card on the bottom of the pile is the first one you were drawn to Shaz"

"Oh and be sure to have any particular question or issue in mind as you select the cards you are drawn towards"

(she will take 13 cards and do as instructed, I then continue by saying)

"Right Shaz, I'm about to explain to you what each of these cards is meant to mean, in other words I'll briefly tell you individually card by card, what most of the books would tell you each of these 13 cards mean and then I will more importantly explain how they uniquely and personally interconnect for you Shaz, is that OK?"

(As I am saying the patter above, I deal the cards into 3 rows of 4, so the top 4 cards are closest to me, the next 4 go in the middle, next 4 closet to the person having the reading and the odd 13th Card is set off to one side, I'll come back to this later)

"So Shaz, Please Remember NOT to Tell me anything, I'd sooner go through all the cards and tell you what they mean, then how they uniquely connect and what they personally mean for you, then at the very end, then and only then I will ask you if any or ALL OF IT MAKES SENSE, and at that point we'll find out if your questions have been answered by the Tarot Or not, does that make sense?"

(She will answer Yes, they always do, oh and hypnotically this sentence has the embedded command that **ALL OF IT MAKES SENSE** and also contains the law of reversed effort suggestion of NOT thus meaning the harder they try not to tell you stuff, the more likely they are to do so without even realising it)

"However Shaz, if as occasionally happens something confuses me or I'm not picking up on the energies strongly enough, then I may ask you a direct question, but it will be one that can be answered YES or NO, and should I do so, then please just answer YES or NO, I don't want any clues and I don't want anybody thinking that you told me everything! OK Shaz, does that all make Sense?"

(She will say Yes, Yet Again, they always do)

Right at this point things are stacked in your favour, so lets clarify a few other things. In the information above the 4 cards laid closest to client I refer to as being Past, the Middle ones Present and those closet to me Future, with the extra 13th card set to one side being an indicator card that will help tie everything together and make sense of it all.

With that in mind there are 13 cards on the table so using the memory system in the audio earlier, you can easily talk for anywhere from around 6 ½ minutes (30 Seconds a card) up to 26 minutes (2 minutes a card), just by telling them what each individual card means by way of the memory system triggers which will prompt off ideas in your head of what to say and also by describing to them the things you saw in the cards when doing the Tarot Card Meditation I spoke of earlier.

Whilst doing this I am at all times paying attention to their body language looking out for them nodding their head (yes) or shaking it (no) and also looking for them fidgeting as if something I just said has related to something that made them feel uneasy.

In short observe and then later you can say what you see and what you saw, more often than not what you picked up on will be correct.

This observation and also listening out for noises of recognition will usually give you all you need for the rest of the reading where you tie it all together and then recap emphasising the Facts and stuff that really resonated and made sense to them and seemed real accurate by the responses they give you.

I say by the responses they give you, as always without fail, at this stage when I've explained what each of the cards mean, I start to weave a story of how they link together with each other, and without fail I will part way through after having said a few things suddenly stop, pause, look her in the eye and say

"Shaz, I'm feeling really odd energies, a kind of confusion, is some of this making sense to you Shaz?"

Yes its a blatant question, but she will either come back and tell you why its making sense or why its not, if she just says Yes you know your on the right track, if however she just says no you can respond,

"Umm I didn't so much mean what the cards are telling me Shaz, as more would a sense of confusion about the question or issue you had in mind make any sense to you right now?"

This prompts her to open up and talk, giving valuable clues away about where to guide the reading as you then go back to explain how all the cards interconnect with each other in a personal and unique way for her.

At the apparent end of the reading, having fed back to her the things I've picked up on from her Verbal and Non Verbal Reactions to what I have been saying and also those things that my observation and common sense of for example what she is wearing, what names are visible on any Tattoos or Jewellery and all the usual things of that nature, I will then say:

"So does that all make sense to you Shaz?"

(She has to say Yes as prior to asking the question at this point all I have done is tell her things which I have already established are right)

"And with that in mind before we end for today, is there any other specific question you'd like to ask the cards"

(If she says NO you've done a killer reading and job, however many times they will have just one more question and when they do I continue and say)

"OK Shaz, well as we're running out of time, please just state out loud what that question or issue is that you want advice from the cards for and select 3 cards as you do so"

(She says it out loud and picks 3 cards, at which point I answer using common sense and in a manner that will make her feel positive and upbeat)

Now I know some of you will be thinking, that will never work, they'll never fall for that, but honestly I've been doing readings since 1989, and I regularly was getting rebooked by the same people time and time again when I choose to concentrate on this field.

They sent bookings galore my way through word of mouth and always insisted to their friends that **THEY NEVER TOLD ME ANYTHING**.

Indeed they often insist on making the point that **I TOLD THEM TO TELL ME NOTHING AND NOT GIVE ME ANY CLUES.**

And as the vast majority of Psychics don't say a statement such as that, especially not with the built in psychological wording, which basically is such that the way things are worded makes them more likely to want to tell you as you've told them not to!

Oh and another secret, read the above again and you'll notice that right at the start I stare directly into her eyes, go silent and extend my hand to shake hers, this is unexpected by her, and thus arguably, immediately induces a light trance state, it what they call a pattern interrupt.

From that moment on I tend to talk in a Hypnotic Tone of Voice and stare directly into her eyes whenever talking, or at least it seems that way, in truth I am staring at the bridge of her nose so she will always be the first one to break eye contact.

Oh and when you read it all again, pay attention to how often I steer things so she has to say YES which gets her into a "Yes Set" state of mind and more likely to open up and positively reconstruct reality in your favour.

Then at the end of the reading when I am feeding back all the stuff I have established to be true, accurate and correct, I will vary my tone of voice and become more upbeat and louder in tone of voice...

Some would argue this awakens her from the trance and embeds only the positive information into her mind, thus eliminating any memory of the clever questioning that actually did take place.

However this is not a book on Hypnosis, although honestly I would advise anyone wishing to become a more powerful and successful Psychic Reader to learn Hypnosis and to that end may I suggest you search my name Jonathan Royle on your local magic dealers website?

Another Ploy I will use most every time I do a reading is to part way into the reading, go silent for a minute or two and stare intently at all the cards, picking some up for a closer look and making the odd "umm ha ha" kind of noises to give the impression that something is starting to make more sense to me.

After having done this for a minute or so (which seems much longer and builds up the clients expectations) I will then say something such as:

"Wow Shaz, you know sometimes when I am doing readings, sometimes I truly hope that I am wrong in what I am seeing in the cards and what I am sensing that they truly mean to you, as to be honest I'd sooner be seeing or sensing things wrong than it to be true that you've had this situation going on around you! Does that Make Sense Shaz?"

(When I was staring at all the cards I will have been conjuring up a story in my mind of a nature that is perceptively negative, ready to relate it to the client after I have delivered the above line which she will most likely react to in a manner that will give me tons of information (either verbally or non verbally) to have a real good idea of any negative stuff that may have been going on or that she fears may be about to go on)

"So with that in mind Shaz, as I say I hope I'm wrong with this, as to be honest I'm not entirely sure as there is a sense of confusion as to whether this is directly related to you, or is more a message relevant to somebody who is close to you – does that make sense?"

(You now just given yourself the perfect out and escape route)

*At this point I relate the story I have made up in my head based on weaving a story together based on the meanings of each of the cards, at all times looking out for nods or shakes of the head so I can steer off or stay on track as needed.

*More often then not you'll get amazing results and tons of hits that will even surprise you, but if for some reason the client does not make sense of it then you can always say:

"Well Shaz, I did say I hoped I was wrong, so I am relieved its not making direct sense to you, but to be honest the feelings I am getting are growing much stronger so I am not going to take back or change anything I have said based on what I can see and feel, actually its becoming more clear to me now, that this is more of a message to keep your eyes and ears open around close family and friends as this is going to be relevant in the near future to one of them and you'll find unexpectedly that your one of the main keys in helping them to overcome all of this successfully! Does that make sense Shaz?"

You'll find more often than not tough, that you'll be more accurate and on target than you could possibly ever imagine!

Finally and In closing, please allow me to remind you that we are all **BASICALLY THE SAME AS HUMAN BEINGS..** (although we all pretty much want to believe and feel we are different and unique)

Cold Reading & Mentalism For The Psychic Entertainer

I shall now share some extracts from another of my previous books entitled "Cold Reading & Mentalism For The Psychic Entertainer" which is available in ebook format from **https://sellfy.com/p/dcbu/** or in Paperback Book format by visiting either Amazon USA **http://tinyurl.com/mtv6ehf** or Amazon UK **http://tinyurl.com/mgqyvjj**

Or for those of you who prefer Hard Back books you can order a copy in Hard Back Format from **http://www.lulu.com/spotlight/royle1057**

These random extracts that follow all contains "Secrets" and "Insights" that are extremely relevant to conducting effective demonstrations of Clairvoyance and/or Spiritual Healing.

Make much of your patter about Predictions for the FUTURE, as these cannot be disproved at the time of the reading. Whereas you give very sketchy details of past events you can see via their navels – here for future predictions be very detailed, very precise and very enthusiastic about what you are saying – also use a little common sense. By this I mean that although future events cannot be proved or disproved until a later time, with a little common-sense you can get well over 50% of your future predictions correct as most people experience similar things in their life at one time or another.

Don't forget also that before appearing on TV/Radio shows or Live Shows with guest Celebrities or indeed before meeting these people for other Media interviews you would have been told who your subjects were going to be.

It is then a simple job to get onto the internet and visit some of that Celebrities fan club sites which quite often contain lots of little known information about the person, their past, their present and their future plans!

On many occasions I've acquired information on Celebrities which I am to meet the following day from Internet gossip sites and fan sites and then have fed this information to them by way of my Belly Button reading predictions.

More often than not the detailed nature of what I have then been revealing has stunned the celebrities in question and on one memorable occasion I told a famous female American pop star what the name of her next album would be (I'd seen lots of rumours on fan/gossip sites) and she was so amazed that she admitted that although it was not public knowledge (she must not have seen the websites) that she would admit this was correct. So don't underestimate the power of the Internet for obtaining information on clients for use in your Psychic Readings!

Remember to say very little – but appear to say a lot. This is easy to do by using lots of long and detailed words, phrases and descriptions to describe something, which is actually very simple, and either applies to everybody or to most people at some time in their lifes.

For example I use phrases like "You've lost a little bit of your sparkle recently haven't you love?" If she says Yes I would continue "Yes I know you have, you've been feeling down haven't you?" – well here she's bound to say Yes as your only saying the same thing in a different way again!

Then Continue "Yes you've been worrying a lot – then worrying about worrying it's become a viscous circle but its about to end and life will be like a bed of roses again in the very near future – you will keep positive won't you love?" – again she'll say Yes so you sound to be getting things 100% Correct!

But look at what I said again and you'll see one of my favourite Cold reading techniques in action which is to say something which is detailed but then end it with a positive closed question which can only really be answered YES by the subject as to answer YES is in their own interest!

Answering yes to this closed question has nothing to do with whether the predictions and information contained within the rest of that sentence were correct or not – however the audience watching or listening will perceive the subjects answers of YES as validation that your statements and predictions are correct!

Obviously if she answered No to the very first question you'd shoot off in the opposite direction and say something like "Well I know you don't feel like you've lost any of your sparkle but others have noticed your working too hard – you will take a little more time for yourself from now on won't you love?"

Here once again the closed question technique is used and once again it's in her interest to answer Yes – don't underestimate this cold reading technique its very useful indeed.

Furthermore, the more often you can get your subjects to say YES to you – the far less likely they are to either say you are wrong or indeed to even let the thought that you may be or are wrong enter their head – it is in effect mild brainwashing.

I always start readings by making it quite clear that "Whenever I ask you a question I want you to answer Loud and clear!" (Pause) "Just say YES nice and loud! – OK?"

This is perceived by them and the audience as telling them to answer clearly to questions – but at a subconscious level in their mind prompts them to answer YES to everything.

This may sound like fairytale stuff – but I've been using techniques like this for the past 15+ Years since I started doing Stage Clairvoyance shows like Doris Stokes and other famous mediums in 1990 aged 15 years old and these methods have always worked for me!

Next we'll discuss the use of Closed questions just a little bit more before explaining how I use the power of Open Ended Statements and Questions for Cold Reading Success.

Closed Questions are those which can easily be answered by just saying Yes or No, and as in the aforementioned examples these can be phrased so that it is in the interest of the subject to answer Yes.

To repeat what I've already said only moments ago, for which I make no apologies as this is one of the strongest ploys you can have as a Professional cold reader – closed questions can be used to make your readings seem super accurate.

This technique is especially useful to Psychics doing Live demonstrations on TV & Radio shows and also to Stage Clairvoyants who perform before a large audience.

To re-iterate what I've said already, deliver a long list of detailed sounding (yet quite general) predictions and apparently factual pieces of information to the subject and then end your rather long winded sentence with a closed question to which it is in their interest to answer Yes.

Then as everyone hears them reply YES, they perceive this as being the subject validating all the things you have said as correct when in truth they are merely answering the question which you ended your statement with.

Another example of a closed question being used in this way is as follows "With my finger in your navel I'm being shown a picture of a Valley made up of lots of hills and this is symbolic of your life to date!"

"The hills are in various sizes and I believe this is showing me the ups and downs you've had throughout your life – You're a survivor aren't you?"

(Its in their interests to say Yes as its good for their ego/pride to do so)

"Now I'm being shown a picture of a brick wall and I feel this is symbolic of the wall you put around you in new encounters with people – You've been hurt in the past when you've least expected it haven't you?"

(This will be answered Yes as we all have been at one time or another – yet it sounds to all listening like this is a truly detailed revelation you're making!)

"Now I'm being shown you caught between the devil and the deep blue sea so to speak – I'm being shown an image of you stuck between two people"

"Now both these people are friends, they may be in a relationship together, but what is clear to me is that you have become piggy in the middle to them because you don't want to upset anyone. Would I be right in saying you don't like upsetting people especially your friends?" (who is going to say anything else other than Yes you are right?)

"Yes I can see it clearly, there are two people around you, it may be family but I'm more inclined to say its on a friendship level. And both of these two people have been asking for your advice – yes that's it you don't want to take sides with either of them as you value the friendship of them both. You do value your close friendships don't you?" (Again Yes will be the answer)

"I can see good things for you in the future, I'm being shown prosperous times ahead for you. In fact I'd go so far too say that your going to come into some money soon. Those things you have been dreaming of aren't so far away now you'll be getting them sooner than you think – You've had your mind set on something very special to you for several years haven't you?

(we all have dreams/ambitions so the answer will be Yes)

I could go on for pages and pages, in fact for days and days with examples of how closed questions can be used at the end of statements of apparent fact and can be phrased so as to guarantee a positive Yes response but I would hope that the examples I have given will set you on the right track and get you devising ones of your own.

Next lets turn our attention to the use of Open ended statements and questions and how these can be used by the Psychic to obtain far more information from the client about their life and problems than even they realise they are giving you!

Then later on in the reading this information which they have freely given you without even realising how much they have said can be fed back to them in a different context and/or phrased differently and will be accepted by them as amazing insights from you into their life/problems!

Quite simply an Open ended Statement is a statement, which could mean almost anything and cannot really ever be pinned down as meaning just one thing – hence its meaning is OPEN! And Open ended questions are quite simply questions which are phrased in such a manner that they cannot be answered by just a Yes or No response and will instead provoke the subject to give you a detailed answer and therefore far more information than you actually really asked for or they realise giving you.

An example of an open ended statement would be: "I feel that at times you get very stressed and yet in other situations you are a very calm, relaxed and peaceful person."

This is neither right nor wrong for anybody! It will always be seen as being right as both possible scenarios and options are contained within the same statement of apparent fact!

Therefore the fact the statement cannot be seen as either right or wrong makes it OPEN and so it will fit everyone in some way at some time and so people will always respond as though it is CORRECT!

In other words Open statements are ones where you tell the subject they are one thing and then tell them they are at times the direct opposite as well!

Or you tell them they feel an emotion in certain situations and then tell them the direct opposite of this situation/emotion within the same statement.

I hope you get the hang of it as Open statements are a very easy way of devising Cold Reading patter which will fit every person on this planet or as it is known in the Cold reading trade "Boiler-Plate".

Open ended questions are those which cannot be answered with just a Yes or a No such as these few examples which follow:

"Why do I keep being shown images of a property matter in my minds eye?"

(They cannot possibly answer with just a simple Yes or No to a question such as this and instead will have to give a more detailed answer. If they are involved with some kind of property matter then they will tell you exactly what it is and later on in the reading you can feed this information back to them in a different context – perhaps with reassuring words that all things regarding this matter will prove successful! However if they state that they have no knowledge of a property matter you would very easily steer off on another course as follows)

"To be honest it doesn't surprise me that as yet you are not aware of this property matter (this implies there will be one soon) however I can see this image so clearly that I can very confidently predict that within the next six months period property matters will become an important focus in your life. I'm being told to warn you to consider all the options when this occurs and not rush in like a bull in a China shop! You will be careful when this happens won't you?"

Well that's one example of how to phrase an open ended question which as with all open ended questions will make one of two things happen, either:

A) They will have something going on in their life which relates to the subject matter to which you are asking the question (asking for more information) and this they will then freely explain to you in great detail as they feel you are already aware of it – or why else would you have asked the question? Then later in this same reading this information is fed back to them in different words.

B) Or they will have no knowledge of such matters raised – but will instead usually make you aware of other matters in their life of concern to them as part of their answer and this itself gives you information which you can return to later in the reading. You then turn this into a prediction for the future and as such either way it will only ever seem like an accurate statement/prediction on your part!

Another ploy to make the reading more accurate is to half way through your predictions and comments ask the subject if they have any specific questions they would like you to try and answer?

Just say to them "Well I'm seeing so much in your Navel and we have so little time together today so to speed things up for you, are there any specific questions or areas of your life you'd like me to look into?"

This makes it sound innocent enough, you don't seem like your probing for help and needless to say their answers give you all the information you need to carry on the reading in a very specific and accurate manner.

Two last points on Navel Cold Reading and these are that

a) whether you are a believer in genuine intuition and Psychic powers or not – please do trust your intuition. The method of seeing a blank TV screen in your mind and allowing images to pop onto it as mentioned earlier in this manual is not only a good piece of explanatory patter – BUT IT ALSO WORKS!

OK so you might think I'm bonkers, but if I had a pound for every time I've been on TV and suddenly said the first thing that came into my head of a very detailed and specific nature with 100% CORRECT & SUCCESSFUL RESULTS – then I'd be rich!!!

b) Secondly don't forget that other options are also open to you in order to make a really good impression on very important TV shows such as the use of a Mentalists Impression Clipboard before the show goes on air!

You could get the people who are to have their Navels read to write down on a slip of paper three things: 1) The most important memory they have from their past. 2) The most important thing going on in their life at present. 3) Their biggest dream/ambition for the future.

They are told this is being done, as it will help make things clearer in THEIR MINDS and EASIER FOR THEM when you get on air! In other words it is portrayed that you've had them do this FOR THEIR BENEFIT!

You then tell them to fold up the slips which you make clear you have not seen (you can see what the clipboard says later!) and to hide them in one of their pockets as you WILL NOT be using these on air – no they have just been written out by the subjects to get things CLEAR IN THEIR MINDS.

The subjects will not think anything strange of this especially as you will make the main part of their readings up from Cold Reading methods, but along the way for each subject you can reveal thanks to the clipboard one very definite and very detailed item about their Past, Present & Future.

You end up looking amazing, the viewers or live show audience are never any the wiser about the use of the clipboard before the show, and best of all Belly Button Reading and your talents in the use of it look super accurate and so even more FREE TV/Radio, Newspaper & Magazine publicity can easily be obtained.

With reference to the use of a Mentalists clipboard to obtain information for your reading please refer to the psychology behind how I use one for Pawology in a later chapter of this manual!

The Questionnaire which you get them to fill in on the Mentalists clipboard could also contain the disclaimer for "Navel-Healing" which will be mentioned shortly whilst also asking for their contact details for use in further media features.

NAVEL-HEALING

Next we shall turn our attention to Navel Healing or as it is also called Belly Button Psychic Healing.

Again this is based on The Native American Indians beliefs and religion of Shamanism, along with the seven energy points in our body called Chakras.

Once again the Base Chakra which is in line with the Human Navel is used, except this time it is used for the purposes of powerful Spiritual Healing.

To help heal someone's complaints once they have first been to see a conventional Doctor (as we neither diagnose nor prescribe) we use a small pointed Quartz Crystal, which is placed into their Belly Button in order to promote natural healing!

One end of the Quartz Crystal is placed into their Navel and the other end held by the fingertips of your left hand and then your positive psychic healing energy is directed through your body, into the crystal and then into the Base Chakra energy point in order to promote rapid healing.

The reason this works so successfully is akin to the beliefs of many other complementary medicines such as Acupuncture, within which the Chinese practitioners believe that all illnesses, diseases and mind/body defects are caused by energy imbalances within the person's body.

Therefore logic states that if we feed positive healing energy into the patients most powerful psychic energy point (The Base Chakra) that this will help correct those imbalances and as such lead to successful recovery in rapid time!

The use of the pointed Quartz crystal as a way to get some of your positive healing energy into the patient is for two reasons.

Firstly the Quartz Crystal itself is used extensively in other forms of New Age Medicine such as Crystal Healing and indeed it is openly known by the majority of the public how powerful Quartz Crystal's actually are and the power they do in reality contain. This is a genuine tangible power which they contain and is the reason why small pieces of Quartz Crystal are placed into the mechanics of most all watches, as it is proven that the 100% NATURAL ENERGY within them helps the watch run better.

Also in much the same way THE NATURAL ENERGY of the Quartz Crystal helps the Human Body to run better, hence many people wear jewellery containing Quartz Crystal as a preventative health measure.

Here in Navel-Reading the Quartz crystal is used to help accelerate THE NATURAL HEALING process!

The reason why one end is stuck into the patients Navel whilst you hold the other end with the fingertips of your left hand is twofold.

Firstly The Crystal helps to amplify the power and intensity of the healing energy which is sent from our body into the patients and Secondly by holding the Crystal with the left hand things are amplified even more as it is the left side of the brain which deals with all things Spiritual and Psychic.

Once the Crystal is in position in the patients Navel you have them close their eyes and imagine a feeling of warmth starting to enter their body which is symbolised by the colour orange in their minds eye.

You explain that just so long as they concentrate on this feeling of warmth and keep seeing the colour Orange brightly in their minds eye that healing will prove successful for them. (This also puts the blame onto them if successful results do not occur as planned – you just blame it on their lack of concentration)

The Logic of getting them to focus on a warm feeling is quite simply that people do naturally feel better within themselves when they are warm.

And the reason you get them to see the colour Orange brightly in their minds eye is both because seeing it brightly is as proven in NLP a positive thing and positive thoughts lead to positive results, but also is because the colour Orange is a powerful combination of the colours Red & Yellow mixed together and as such is the most powerful colour of the spectrum.

Then you the Healer concentrate on a blue beam of light energy flowing from all the seven energy points (Chakras) in your body, down through your left arm/hand and into the Crystal before finally entering the patients body via their Base Chakra energy point.

You concentrate on Blue energy/light as this is the curative healing energy – Just think of The Blue Cross emergency service for animals and you'll remember this easily.

Results will often be instantaneous, although they are always told this IS NOT an alternative to conventional medicine and rather is COMPLEMENTARY medicine, which just helps to dramatically speed up the healing process.

(This statement covers you both legally and morally and ensures that they seek conventional medical treatment and/or continue with any prescribed medication until a conventional Doctor says otherwise)

However results will often be dramatic and instant or within a very short space of time (which can still be used for follow up media coverage by keeping a mailing list of all participants in your show that receive Navel Healing).

The reason success so often occurs so rapidly is because of the proven fact that 90% of all reported illness is psychosomatic (all in their mind with no physical cause) and it is probable that 100% of unreported illness is also psychosomatic.

In these cases of Psycho-Somatic illness, as the illness is being caused by the patients mind – so the cure lies in their mind also, hence it is true to say that if they believe this will work for them THEN IT WILL.

Those that believe will naturally set their mind to a different way of thinking and so the end result can be one of an often apparently miraculous Cure.

Combine this with the PLACEBO EFFECT, which again all comes down to the patient BELIEVING that the treatment will work and you can now see why Psychic Belly Button Healing can be so successful.

This success combined with the perceptively bizarre method of treatment is what will attract all the TV/Radio, Newspaper and Magazine interest as it has done extensively for me in the past.

To understand both how Navel-Gazing & Navel-Healing can be and are so successful may I strongly urge you to buy or rent the excellent film "Leap of Faith" starring Steve Martin as this film is almost a course in itself of how Psychic Readings and Healing are achieved with successful results and as Steve Martins Character says in the film:

"To answer your question of if I'm genuine or fake I say this, what's it matter how I do things – Just so long as the job gets done!"

This is a sentiment I agree with entirely and just so long as you get a signed declaration from any patients you treat with Navel Healing which states:

1) They agree (if they haven't already) to get a conventional Medical Doctors diagnosis and prescription as soon as possible.

2) They agree to continue seeing their conventional Medical Doctor and/or continue taking any medication which they may have been prescribed.

3) They agree to allow you to touch their Belly Button for the purposes of Healing. (This covers you from any potential assault charges!)

You are then covered both legally and morally as you will never be placing a patient into any danger and instead have their best interests at heart always.

This signed disclaimer also asks for their contact details and acts as your mailing list for people to contact for inclusion in future media features on Navel-Healing.

Their recovery will most times prove to be considerably faster after Navel Healing than if they had just had conventional treatment alone and again this is because of their BELIEF that it will help them which in itself can REVERSE many problems which were Psycho-Somatic (Psychologically induced).

One of the Key phrases I use is "Those of you with health problems who volunteer tonight will only receive truly successful healing IF YOU WANT IT TO WORK (in other-words if you believe) and if you use your powers of Intelligence, imagination and Concentration effectively!"

This Psychologically ensures that only those who BELIEVE that rapid healing will result will volunteer and indeed as such these in my experience usually tend to be the ones for whom it will work.

This Phrase also covers you for failure as if instant healing does not occur, which often cannot be proved one way or the other until the patient revisits their doctor, then the way it is phrased puts the blame for failure onto the patient.

You see the audience will just see it as failure on the patient's part for not using their powers of intelligence, imagination and concentration effectively as they were told to do!

It is in effect A FORM OF HYPNOSIS, except with Navel healing the patient HYPNOTISES THEMSELVES due to their own belief system telling them that this form of treatment will work for them!

IF THEY BELIEVE IT WILL BE SO – THEN SO IT WILL BE

Well that basically is all there is to Navel-Healing as the rest is just down to presentation on your part. Present Navel-Healing with NO DOUBTS in your mind that it will work and then this positive attitude will be sensed by your volunteers.

When your volunteers sense this confident attitude within you that Navel Healing will be beneficial to them then they will start to be even more positive about it working and so the magic of Positive Thinking comes into play.

And need I remind you of the countless books published and medical studies done on Positive thinking which have proved beyond doubt that positive thinking can often lead to CURES in and of itself.

So with the combination of Positive Thinking, Self-Belief of the patient, The placebo Effect, Self-Hypnosis and Psychic Mumbo Jumbo all combined into one treatment method, Navel-Healing is very powerful indeed.

Usually Navel-Healing would be done with the person there in person next to you, however for TV/Radio phone ins and media articles (or mail order sales) this can be got around by using a good clear photograph of the persons Navel.

The theory as to why this will still work regards the photo is the same as with Navel-Reading, however here you also speak to them in person over the phone and step by step explain what you are doing at your end.

It is also explained to the patient what they must do at their end as you concentrate the healing energy through the crystal into the photo of their Navel and due to some of the energy of their Base Chakra being caught in the Photo, then into their body for the same healing results.

This is known as "distance healing" and just so long as the patient believes it will work, then it will prove to be just as successful as if the person was next to you in person.

I will now explain a few visual demonstrations which can be used on TV and Live stage shows to demonstrate instantly how successful the technique of Navel-Healing is, and may I point out that if these demonstrations are carried out BEFORE any actual personal one to one healing is done then results will be INCREASED!

The reason quite simply being that once the patients to be have seen these visual demonstrations of how Navel-Healing works, then their BELIEF & FAITH in it working for them will be total.

WEAK ARM – STRONG ARM TEST

This is a visual demonstration which I have used along with the other tests which will be explained with great success in the past on TV shows including "Psychic Livetime" (Granada Breeze), "Live at Three" (UK Living) and Children's "Nickelodeon" TV Station amongst many others.

I have also used it extensively as a live demonstration piece both on Stage & in Cabaret and also whilst giving lectures at many of the Psychic Fairs which in the past I have attended and exhibited at!

EFFECT

Volunteer one clenches their right fist and then with their fist in this closed position places their right arm outstretched straight in front of them.

They are told to close their eyes and imagine clearly a time in their life when they felt very weak unloved & unwanted.

They are told to now notice how weak, how drained and how NEGATIVE this makes them feel.

"Feeling weak, drained and negative from the tips of your toes to the tips of your fingers!"

You tell them to TRY to keep their arm straight out in front of them as they allow these NEGATIVE emotions and feelings to flood their entire body from tip to toe.

Then you count to three: - 1,2, and on 3 you cue a 2nd volunteer upon the stage to push down the first persons right arm which they find they are able to do with the greatest of ease.

It is explained to the audience that under normal circumstances the 1st volunteer would have been able to keep his arm much stiffer, much straighter and out in front of him for much longer despite volunteer number two pushing down on his arm.

It is explained that this demonstrates how Negative emotions in our minds can lead to Negative effects in our bodies and as a consequence often lead to unnecessary illnesses and disease.

The good news however, is that by using a form of treatment such as Navel Healing we can remove all negative emotions from our bodies and therefore end up with a far more healthy life.

To demonstrate this you have Volunteer number 1 close their eyes once again, you place the Quartz Crystal into their Belly Button and have them imagine the warmth represented by the colour Orange that is now flooding into their body.

They are told that just so long as they see the colour Orange clearly that in a few moments time something which was just a few moments ago so difficult will now become so ridiculously easy to achieve.

They are told to notice the inner strength they now feel which is making each and every muscle group in their body from the tips of their toes to the tips of their fingers STRONGER than they have ever been before.

(You of course during this time also appear to do your bit of directing energy into their Base Chakra energy point whilst thinking of the Blue Healing energy!)

Volunteer number one is then told to resume the same position as before with their right fist clenched and their right arm held outstretched straight in front of them.

Volunteer number two is then told "OK on the count of three just TRY to push his arm down and notice how difficult it is for you and how much STRONGER he has become, 1, 2, 3, That's it just TRY to push down his arm.

Volunteer number two is allowed to continue TRYING for a few seconds or so and then is told to relax. Then volunteer one is told to relax also and take their new-found strength with them.

When asked volunteer one WILL SAY how weak he felt the first time and indeed how much stronger he felt the second time around.

Volunteer two when asked will genuinely comment how much more difficult she found it to get his arm to budge the second time around.

EXPLANATION

Everything is done and carried out 100% exactly as I have just explained, with only a few points being of particular relevance as follows:

The first time around volunteer one has to hold their arm out in front of them from the very start of the demonstration and so it is little wonder that their arm is tired by the time volunteer two comes to push it down.

Also the first time around the psychological effect of thinking of negative things will genuinely make volunteer one feel weaker – its quite simply a simple form of SELF-HYPNOSIS which makes this work without fail with any willing & co-operative subject.

The suggestion of "TRY to keep your arm out straight in front of you!" suggests by that single word TRY that they will be unable to do so!

This is a technique known in Hypnosis as "The Law of Reversed Effort" which states that the harder they TRY to do something the less success they will have!

And finally with reference to the first time round where volunteer one is made to feel weak, because you cue volunteer two to push their arm down on the count of three without person one hearing you it will then come as a shock when it happens!

Because volunteer one does not know when his arm will be pushed down or indeed expect it to happen at all, it will be a complete surprise to him when this happens, he will be caught off-guard and will not have chance to tense up his by now already very tired arm.

The moment this first demonstration is done both volunteers are told to relax as normal. This gives volunteer one time to rest his arm ready for the second time!

This time volunteer one stands with his arms by his side and eyes closed as you tell him to think of the positive times in his life when he felt STRONG, confident and on top of the world.

He is told to notice that as he clearly sees these things in his minds eye so at the same time he starts to feel STRONGER in each and every muscle group from the tips of his toes to the tips of his fingers.

You then start to explain to the audience that its time to make volunteer one much stronger and healthier by the power of Navel Healing and go into the usual Psychic Mumbo Jumbo at this point!

The moment volunteer one has started to visualise the colour Orange clearly in their mind, then and only then you get them to resume their original position of having their right arm straight out in front of themselves with the fist clenched.

Volunteer one is told "Notice how much stronger you feel, notice how much stronger you are and how much stronger you have become!"

Volunteer two is then told "On the count of three I want you to TRY and push his arm down as you did before, except this time notice how much harder it becomes for you to achieve this."

Then you count 1,2, and on 3 – Just TRY to push down his hand, that's it Just TRY, TRY (continue like this for a few seconds and then say) And now everyone just relax once again.

This time volunteer one has been warned when the pushing will begin and has time to tense their arm, also this second time around it is upon volunteer two that the Law of Reversed effort is used by suggesting to her to TRY and push down his hand.

SUMMING-UP

Do exactly what I have just explained in exactly the way I have said to do it and this demonstration will work EVERY time. Yes the levels of success will vary, but in general 9 times out of ten the visual difference will be VERY DRAMATIC!

And in the other 10% of cases it will still be visual enough to show that Navel-Healing has indeed made the man stronger the second time around.

This works due to a combination of The Law of Reversed Effort (TRY), the verbal suggestions given to them and the things they think of (self hypnosis), and the fact that second time around the man (volunteer one) has prior warning of when the woman (volunteer two) will TRY to push down his arm.

He has of course also had a minute or two to rest his arm between tests and this time only places his arm outstretched in front of him at the last second, thus not giving it time to get tired as in the first instance.

This may not sound very impressive when described like this on paper, but visually its very dramatic and makes for a good TV or Stage Show demonstration which both the audience and those whom participate in the experiment will find AMAZING!

BUCKET OF ICE TEST

This is a routine, which I originally saw demonstrated by a so-called Conventional Psychic Healer called Mathew Manning on Uri Geller's ITV Special "Beyond Belief".

EFFECT

It is explained to a volunteer seated on stage, that in a few moments time their right arm will be placed into the fish tank next to them which is full of Cold Water and Ice.

They are told to remove their hand from the Iced Water the very second that they feel it is too cold or painful to keep their hand in it any longer.

They are told to close their eyes and you then lift up their arm and place it into the tank of Iced Water without warning.

From the second their hand enters the Water until the very second they remove their hand is timed by a stopwatch which is held and operated by a 2nd Volunteer from the audience.

The time is noted and Volunteer one is told how long they managed to keep their arm under water before the Navel-Healing begins.

Volunteer One is told to close their eyes and relax as you place the Quartz Crystal into their Navel and start the Psychic Mumbo Jumbo.

You suggest to them that "In a few moments time when and only when I count to 3, then and only then I will place your right arm into the water tank beside you."

"This time you will notice that from the very second your hand enters the water you WILL FEEL calm, relaxed and confident in every way!"

"You will notice that something you once thought would be so difficult now becomes so ridiculously easy and you will feel NO DISCOMFORT whatsoever!"

Then you go into the think of the colour Orange Blurb and feel the warmth Patter mentioning to the volunteer that:

"Just so long as you keep seeing the Colour Orange brightly in your minds eye whilst feeling that warmth flooding your entire body YOU WILL FEEL NO DISCOMFORT whatsoever and will be able to keep your hand in the tank for much longer with the greatest of EASE!"

1- Relaxed, Calm & confident.

2- feeling warm & strong inside and on

3- Just notice how, unlike last time you feel no discomfort whatsoever. (As you count three you place their hand back into the water)

At this point Volunteer number two starts the stopwatch and prepares to stop it the very second that volunteer number one removes their hand from the water again.

The times are compared and it is noticed with much amazement from both those involved and the audience that She was able to keep her hand under water for CONSIDERABLY longer the 2nd time around! She is given a towel to dry her arm and returned to the audience to thunderous applause.

EXPLANATION

Basically if you do exactly what I have explained in the way I have explained it, and say what I have said in the way that I said it then this WILL WORK with great success for you.

The volunteer hypnotises themselves through their belief that Navel Healing will work, as don't forget you asked only for volunteers who were willing & co-operate whilst having very good powers of Intelligence, Imagination and Concentration.

Your suggestions to them as detailed in the "effect" section are worded such as to Hypnotise them further into the belief that this will work.

The fact they have had their hand under the cold water once means that the second time around it is not so much a shock to their system and this alone will allow them to keep their arm under for longer than before.

Also second time around the idea of pain is NEVER allowed to enter their head. You see first time around they are told "Remove your hand from the water the very second it becomes too PAINFUL to keep it there!"

This suggests to them it will be painful and with this in their mind it won't be many seconds before they remove their hand from the water.

However second time around the word pain is NEVER ever mentioned and instead they are told to notice HOW LITTLE DISCOMFORT they will feel and how much easier it will be this time.

Lastly the fact they know how many seconds they kept their hand under first time around will usually make them determined to beat this second time around and in a focused state of mind such as this – SUCCESS WILL BE ACHIEVED. For this experiment I find it works better if the volunteer with the stopwatch is a male whilst a female is used to place her hand into the water tank!

The tank by the way is nothing more than a reasonable sized fish tank, which is filled with 50% cold water, and 50% Ice cubes!

Incidentally it's a proven scientific/medical fact that women have a higher pain threshold than men and that's another reason why I use a woman for this "Bucket of Ice" test.

PSYCHIC STRONGMAN TEST

As a demonstration of Navel-Healing this experiment has been used by me on countless Television shows, and indeed this test is so good that it has been used by top psychic performer Uri Geller on many of his worldwide TV shows to date, although obviously Uri didn't present it as Navel Healing as we will do!

EFFECT

A large volunteer is seated on a stool/chair and four other volunteers are asked onto the stage to participate.

The man on the chair is told to sit upright with his hands on his lap, whilst the four other volunteers are told to interlock the fingers of both hands so that the fingers of the left hand are against the back of their right hand and vice versa.

With their hands interlocked in this position they are then instructed to place their two Forefingers so that they point outwards with their fingertips away from their interlocked hands.

With their hands like this two people are told to place their outstretched forefingers underneath the seated volunteers armpits (one under his left armpit and one under his right).

And the other two volunteers are told to place their outstretched forefingers under the seated mans kneecap area, again one under the left side and one under the right.

On the count of 3 they are all told to TRY and lift the seated man as high as they can noticing as they do how difficult this is to achieve. 1,2,3 – OK just TRY.

They attempt to do this either with no or very little success, which demonstrates how hard the following test, will be to achieve.

The four volunteers who are stood up all overlap their hands in the air so they go, right, right, right, right, left, left, left, left in order so all four people now have their right hands on top of each other in the pile and then their left hands above these!

At this point you place the Quartz Crystal into each person's Navel and get them to concentrate on the Orange Colour and the warm feeling for a few seconds.

As you do this it is suggested to them all that "In a few moments time we are going to lift this man again and this time something you once thought would be so difficult WILL become so ridiculously easy!"

"Just so long as you think of the colour Orange at all times you will find that he becomes as light as a feather and that you become as strong as an Ox!"

"On the count of three I want you to all remove your hands from the pile and put your hands back together as they were before so that your fingers are interlocked onto the backs of your hands with only your Forefingers pointing outwards away from you.

Then immediately resume your positions as before, so your fingertips are under the mans armpits and kneecaps as you had them before and then the very second I shout NOW – that very second YOU WILL LIFT HIM UP with the greatest of ease.

1 – Confident, Calm & relaxed,

2- Strong as an Ox and on

3- Resume your positions this very second. (Allow them all to do so and then say) NOW – Lift him up – higher and higher and higher!

This happens and yes the man is almost thrown through the roof the second time to everyone's amazement, before being returned to his chair.

EXPLANATION

Don't even ask me to explain why this works – but believe me it does! I can honestly say that I've been using this test both on TV and Live Stage shows for a number of years now and it has NEVER gone wrong.

Admittedly the patter I use is worded following the rules of NLP and as such actually does have a positive psychological effect on the volunteers.

However even if you carry out this test without using the patter I've suggested then, as you will find for yourself, this test will still work! The most bizarre thing about this test is that at the end the seated person will swear that they actually felt themselves get lighter, whilst the four other volunteers will swear they felt themselves get much stronger.

Don't underestimate the visual & psychological impact this test has on an audience as I have always found it to be an excellent applause puller, which is long remembered by the crowd!

STUNTS FOR THE MEDIA

In order to become a regular on TV & Radio shows you will need to get the viewers and listeners involved in such a way that the broadcaster will be bombarded with calls about your Psychic Talents and as such will ask you back sooner rather than later.

It is also far easier to get on TV & Radio shows in the first place if you have just appeared in the printed media, a copy of this recently printed article sent to the shows researchers and/or producers by mail, fax or email will often lead to a TV/Radio follow up interview.

If you have ever seen Uri Geller or indeed myself on a TV show then you will already have a good idea of what I mean, but in any case here are some stunts and ideas which can be used to ensure you become a regular face on TV & Radio shows and in the printed media.

This increased media profile will then lead to more live show bookings and ultimately increased performance fees which of course is our desired aim.

RETURN FROM THE DEAD

With this stunt you tell the viewers or listeners at home to get a pen, a blank sheet of paper, an ashtray and a lighter or matches ready as later on they can take part in an experiment to prove that there really is life after death!

Later in the interview you tell the viewers/listeners to write down onto the piece of paper the full name of a deceased relative or friend with whom they would like to make spiritual contact.

They are then told to set fire to the paper and allow it to burn away in the ashtray, whilst at all times looking into the flames produced by the burning paper.

You tell them that just so long as they stare at the flames and concentrate on their loved ones name, they will receive instant spiritual contact from their friend or family member.

You then say "Anyone watching/listening who carry's out this experiment and makes contact with their loved ones please call the station and tell us what happened on (then give their number) and perhaps we will get you on a future show!"

That's it really except to say that as with all stunts of this nature it is best if you DO NOT tell the shows producer, researcher or presenter that you will be doing it as then they cannot possibly do anything to stop it being transmitted (assuming it's a live show).

Also by finding out the shows direct dial telephone number you can instantly (from memory) give this number out to the viewers or listeners and as a result their phone lines will be jammed.

You can guarantee that their phone lines will be jammed for a few reasons:

1) Because you would have around a dozen of your friends and family who are located in different areas of the Country call up and claim to have had a spiritual experience as a result of the experiment.

2) Because members of the public want to be on TV and the Radio and as such will ring up claiming something has happened when it hasn't in the hope that this may lead to their 15 minutes of fame.

3) A small percentage of people will allow their mind to play tricks on them and will genuinely believe that something has happened.

4) Consider that the show probably only has two or three phone-lines & that from the thousands or millions of people watching/listening if only 0.5% of them responded then that would be hundreds of calls and the phone lines would be jammed for hours.

Stunts which prompt the viewing/listening audience to both participate in an experiment and then to call in will always lead to the phone lines being jammed and those who have seen Uri Geller perform on TV will know that he uses this fact to great effect.

The shows producers, researchers & presenters will all be so impressed by the chaos caused and the interest shown in you by their audience that they will make sure they get you back onto their show VERY – VERY – SOON!

This "RETURN FROM THE DEAD" stunt can also be used in printed media publications, again the readers are told to do exactly the same thing and then upon having a spiritual experience they should contact the publication.

The only difference being that in this case you must tell the publication what you are going to do and in the case of Daily newspapers state an actual time that day when they must carry out the experiment.

With magazines which may have a shelf life of up to a month you should mention an actual date and time (towards end of its shelf life) that the experiment should be carried out.

For some reason making a specific time and date when everyone reading the article should carry out the experiment makes it seem all the more believable that something special will happen and if they start to believe this then their mind WILL play tricks on them and something WILL HAPPEN!

URI GELLER LIVES ON!

The idea of this stunt is to use it when you are on a show giving a demonstration of metal bending.

As you hold the Spoon or Fork in your hand you would look into the camera and say "I want everybody at home to really concentrate on this Fork as then our combined energies together will make it bend!"

Then once the Fork has visibly bent and snapped into two pieces (explained elsewhere) you say something such as "Wow all you wonderful people at home must have been concentrating really hard for that to happen!"

"In fact sometimes when people concentrate as hard as that strange things happen in their own homes!"

"Perhaps the cutlery in your Kitchen draw has developed bends or the keys on your key-ring have become distorted"

"Maybe that broken watch has started working again or something else strange has happened whilst you were staring at me on your screen!"

"If anything strange whatsoever has just happened please call and let us know on (their number) as we'd love to hear from you!"

Once again the Psychology behind this stunt as with most stunts of this nature is that as detailed for "RETURN FROM THE DEAD".

CAN YOU READ MY MIND?

You explain to the viewers/listeners that you have drawn a simple drawing of an object onto a piece of paper before the show started and then you sealed it inside an envelope.

You then give that envelope to the shows presenter and tell them to look after it and not open it until next time I appear on the show (this makes the viewers think you have already been invited back!).

"I want the viewers at home to look directly into my eyes (you look straight at camera) or listen closely to my voice (in case of being on radio or for blind viewers) and I will count to three."

"As I count to three concentrate on me and tune into my mind as I shall be trying to project the image I have drawn and sealed into the envelope to you!"

"1 – concentrate,

2 – see that image clearly in your mind now and on

3 – please draw the image you have seen onto the back of a postcard and send it to us at (their address) and in the very near future I'll be back on the show to reveal how many of you got it right!"

There is no secret to this stunt other than you draw a simple drawing of a house like a child would, you know a simple house, with four windows, a door and a chimney.

The law of averages is on your side and the fact is that lots of the people who do reply will get the object right, certainly the 50 or so friends/family who send postcards in on your behalf will be correct and this itself warrants a reappearance on the show.

The way your patter is worded makes it difficult for the show not to rebook you, as their viewers/listeners will want to know if the object drawn by you is the same as the one they received.

And the large quantities of postcards arriving at the station over the next few days will keep your name at the forefront of the producer's minds, proving by the audience's response to the stunt that you were popular with them!

Remember a stunt such as this needs to be pulled without giving any of the shows production team any form of prior warning as otherwise they will try to stop you asking the viewers/listeners to contact them as from previous experience they will be aware of what chaos this causes!

HELP US WIN THE MATCH

In this stunt you display a large Orange coloured Spot to the shows viewers and/or newspaper/magazine readers.

They are told that the spot is Orange as the colour Orange is a powerful combination of the colours Red and Yellow combined.

You further explain that you have energised the Orange spot with your Psychic energy and that if everyone concentrates on it for 30 seconds seeing clearly the result they wish to achieve then it can become 100% Total Reality.

You count to three (when on TV/Radio) and get the audience to concentrate on the Large Orange dot as you say "Concentrate clearly and England will win their important match today!"

This stunt is so adaptable and becomes newsworthy in almost every sporting event that I love it to bits as does Uri Geller who like myself has used this and stunts similar an awful lot in the past!

The fact is in sporting event finals there is also a 50/50 % chance that the outcome you wish will happen and if your side don't win, its not your fault – oh no its down to those people who did not concentrate properly.

STARE INTO MY EYES

The idea behind this is to have the viewers stare into your eyes as you face the camera or to stare into a close up photo of your eyes in the case of media publications as they concentrate on what they wish to achieve and say it out loud three times.

For example this could like the Orange Dot be made newsworthy by linking it in to getting people to try and make their team, side or player win the event.

However you could also use it at such times as National No Smoking Day by telling them to look into your eyes and say loudly and clearly three times "I AM A CONFIDENT, HAPPY, CALM & RELAXED HELATHY NON SMOKER!"

Those people who would have naturally stopped via will power alone will later attribute their success to the fact they stared into your eyes and this could lead to future media coverage as on air or in the article you tell them:

"Those people who have now after looking into my eyes lost all desire for Tobacco or Cigarettes and feel they will now continue to be the confident, happy, calm & relaxed non smoker that they have now become, please contact us on (their number)"

TV & RADIO PSYCHIC READINGS

If you are asked onto a Live TV or Radio shows to give Psychic readings to the viewers or listeners over the telephone then don't panic.

All the Cold reading techniques you'll need to use are explained in the Navel Reading section of this manual.

Also you will find that in the case of TV/Radio shows the callers will be asked what area of their life it is they are calling about and do they have any specific questions to ask the Psychic.

This will be done by the researchers who answer the phones before that caller is put through to you on air and indeed this information will either be in the case of Radio shows displayed on a screen in front of you as the caller is connected or in the case of TV shows will be told to you through your studio ear-piece.

When neither of these things is to occur you quite simply ask the caller "In what area of your life can I help you today?"

This open ended question makes them answer you with a detailed reply which feeds you all the information you will need to, in conjunction with the cold reading methods give a very accurate appearing reading!

In otherwords in the case of TV/Radio phone ins there is far less guesswork required on your part than on many other occasions.

NEWSPAPER/MAGAZINE COLUMN

Dispensing spiritual advice by way of a regular newspaper or magazine column is the easiest form of "Psychic" work there is by far!

All the people mentioned in the column and to whom you are apparently giving Psychic advice would have written to you via the publication telling you exactly what their problem is and asking for your help.

You therefore already know what the problem is and merely need to give a common-sense logical sounding answer with an element of reassurance to the person who sent their question.

With a little initiative you can mention details which the person has revealed to you in their letter as part of your reply to them in such a manner that anyone else reading the article will think you have revealed this information thanks to your Psychic Powers.

OK I know the person who sent the letter will not be fooled by this, but the MAJORITY of people will be! Also don't forget that the person who wrote in will be more interested in hearing your common-sense advice.

Don't forget to make lots of predictions for the future, as these at the time cannot be proved one way or the other and will sound due to the detailed information you give to be precise psychic insights into that persons life.

For columns like this you usually call yourself a Psychic Agony Aunt/Uncle.

FINAL NOTES: I have over the years greatly expanded on "The Psychic Strongman" routine explained earlier, and in the following video you can see me performing it as I do now - **https://youtu.be/9GzSTdbwDgA** and also a far more light hearted and comical version of the routine can be seen in this video which was filmed when I was the warm up act and compère for Italian Mentalist Luca Volpe when he appeared at "Manchester Magic and Mentalism Festival" - **https://youtu.be/xWAqJCb6HPs**

If you'd like the full explanation of how my new routine works and also Legal Performance Rights to perform the routine then you can find these at this link: **https://sellfy.com/p/cuqt/**

Next I would Like to Share With you The Complete Contents of my book "The Astrologers Dream" which would usually cost you $20 from my store here **https://sellfy.com/p/ttl5/** but which is being included within the pages of this book at no extra charge!

Welcome to "The Astrologers Dream"

Within the pages of this short manuscript, I will reveal to you the ways in which I seem to miraculously reveal peoples Star Signs both from the Stage and also in Close-Up Performances or one to one Psychic Readings.

I have been using all these methods for many years with great success, since I started appearing at Psychic Fairs all over the UK back in around

1989.

I am sure you will agree that they hold great potential, and look far cleaner than many other methods, whilst also being far easier to perform as there is no complicated mental maths or similar to be dealt with.

Read and enjoy. I trust you get as much use out of these methods as I have done over the years.

VISIBLE DECEPTION

Would you like to be able to during your act apparently ask 3 random members of the audience to stand up and then one by one be able to tell them exactly what their Star Sign is without any pre-show work, no stooges or instant stooging, no cueing, nothing written down, in fact this looks as close to pure direct real psychic style mind reading as you are ever going to get and you'll also discover how this approach could also be used to reveal other pieces of personal information about "random" volunteers which you could apparently have no logical or possible way of knowing.

As a bonus Royle also reveals how it is possible to turn a randomly chosen audience member into an instant psychic mind reader so they are able to tell three people apparently chosen at random what their Star Signs are! Again no pre-show work and once again a guaranteed audience killer.

VISIBLE DECEPTION – (THE SECRET'S)

In a nutshell the secret to this routine is once again Hoy's Tossed Out Deck (TOD) Principle, except that on this occasion no deck of cards is ever used.

Anyhow take a look at the information that follows about the Twelve Signs of The Zodiac:

THE 12 SIGN'S OF THE ZODIAC

The first thing you need to know is that the 12 signs of the Zodiac are broken down into the four elements of Air, Earth, Fire and Water.

These Four Elements each have 3 of the Zodiac Star Signs belonging to them as follows:

THE ELEMENT AIR:

GEMINI, May 21-June 21,

LIBRA, September 23-October 22,

AQUARIUS, January 20-February 18

THE ELEMENT EARTH:

TAURUS, April 20-May 20,

VIRGO, August 23-September 22,

CAPRICORN December 22-January 19

THE FIRE ELEMENT:

ARIES March 21-April 19,

LEO July 23-August 22,

SAGITTARIUS November 22-December 21

THE ELEMENT WATER:

CANCER, June 22-July 22,

SCORPIO, OCTOBER 23-November 21,

PISCES February 19-March 20

SO WHAT'S THE SECRET?

Well essentially the secret is one of utmost cheek and involves you at the start of your show asking those people in the audience who know they have a star sign which is an Air sign to stand up, they are then told to sit down and this is repeated three more times for Earth, Fire and Water Signs.

This is done under this guise of getting to know the audience and once done is excused away by then choosing some volunteers for the next routine of your show (which in my instance is the Tossed Out Deck & Mobile Phone Routine which you can learn in my other ebooks available from all good magic dealers)

The Secret is to notice where 3 of the same Star Sign Element are sitting in 3 very different areas of the audience and to remember this information for much later in your show.

Then after a suitable time delay you can appear to randomly point at three different people in the audience and ask them to stand up and merely think of their own star-sign.

The fact is that lets say you remember where three people who stood up and identified themselves as Fire Signs were sitting, you now know that the 3 apparently random (as far as audience is concerned) people that you have pointed to and asked to stand up all have fire signs.

As such you need only say something such as (this example being for Fire Signs)

"All three of you please just concentrate on your star-signs but please don't tell me or indeed anyone what they are yet and please don't tell me if I am right or wrong until I ask you to indicate and let us all know the outcome of this impossible experiment"

"The Three Star Sign's that I sense are being transmitted to me and belong to these three wonderful volunteers are, Aries, Leo & Sagittarius"

Yes that's right you just name all 3 of the fire signs and you are guaranteed to have named each of the 3 peoples star-signs who are standing up as you know for a fact due to the bit at the start of the show that all three of them have Fire Signs.

You can then either proceed in the manner I do with the Tossed Out Deck (see my Ebook "Long Distance Mobile Phone Telepathy" or as Wayne Dobson advises for his Tossed Out Deck Routine.

This fly's over the heads of audiences due to the fact that whilst the majority of people seem to know what their own Star-Sign is (especially women) and whilst the Majority of these know if they are Air, Earth, Fire or Water, in general I have found that most people don't know what all the other Star-Signs are or what elements they fall into and as such never realise that you have called out 3 Fire Signs…

Indeed even if they did realise this, they will due to the time delay most likely have forgotten the bit at the start of the show, and even if they do remember that won't logically see that as being the Secret as quite frankly they won't think you'd be that cheeky.

This really is one of those times where bare cheek, combined with a time delay so that people forget truly does create mind blowing miracles and reactions that are unequalled from your audiences, but don't take my word for it, go out there and try this during a live show and prove to yourself what an amazing reaction it does indeed get!

To apparently enable an onstage volunteer to reveal the three Star-Signs simply take a newspaper and put a black marker pen circle around the three Fire Sign's (as per this example, obviously it could be any of the other elements instead) and then allow a marker pen to dry out so that it does not work any longer.

In performance apparently place an on stage volunteer into an Instant Hypnotic Trance State for which genuine and trickery methods are explained in my book "Confessions of a Hypnotist"

Then hand then the newspaper which you explain is opened to the Horoscopes Page, and also hand them the dried out marker pen and tell them to place both behind their back and then when they get the urge to draw a circle or cross with the pen then to nod their head.

This is repeated two more times and to the audience it appears as if they have on 3 occasions drawn a cross or circle using the marker pen onto the horoscopes page of the newspaper.

In truth when they are brought back round out of the apparent Hypnotic Trance State, the marks or crosses that they will find nearest to 3 Zodiac Signs on the page are ones that you marked earlier due to the pen not working but neither the on stage volunteer or audience know this.

Therefore you can then ask the on stage volunteer to read out the three star signs that they feel the crosses or circles they have drawn are nearest to, which of course will in this example be the three fire signs and as you pointed at and got 3 people to stand up who you know from the start of the show are all fire signs you will suddenly have what appears to the audience to be an absolute miracle on your hands as all 3 of these people sit down and confirm by doing that the on stage volunteer has somehow managed to read all 3 of their minds and mark the 3 correct Zodiac Signs on the newspaper page using the marker pen, which of course as we now know does not actually work!

(This Dried Marker Audience member reveals someone's Zodiac Sign idea I first saw performed and explained at a lecture by Kennedy (Ken Dyne) to whom special thanks must be extended and who's Mentalism Products I cannot praise highly enough)

At this point you ask the audience to give the on stage volunteer a round of applause and as they do just before you send them back to the audience you can ask them directly the question "What's your date of Birth".

This person now returns to the audience and a little later on in the show you could appear to point at them and ask them to stand up, whilst an on stage volunteer stares into their eyes and apparently reads their mind and tells them not only their star sign but also their exact date of birth.

Basically you will have secretly cued the on stage volunteer using the "Klear Thoughtz" principle (See My Ebook By That Name - **https://sellfy.com/p/kxfC/**) and they will have just said the information that you have cued them with, namely the other persons Star Sign and exact date of birth.

You of course in truth got the person who was on stage earlier in the show to blatantly tell you this information under the cover of the audience applauding them as they were sent back to their seats and have then left a time delay for memories of everyone to get distorted.

Then when another audience member later in the show appears to tell someone else in the audience their Star Sign and also their exact date of birth the audience will be absolutely stunned.

The principle of getting the information from the person on stage earlier in the show under the cover of applause then having it revealed in a manner where the audience perceive it as being some kind of amazing mind reading because they don't ever realise that the person just told you is known in Mentalism as "The Dunninger Ploy"

And the fact that the audience perceives this as a true miracle, whilst the person who was on stage earlier is just amazed because they will wonder how the other audience member got to know this information (even though they will remember telling you it earlier) whilst the person on stage will just be amazed about how you were able to cue them the right information to reveal when in their minds there is no way you could of known it is an example of what is known as "Dual Reality" and "Multiple Realties" at work.

Once you have learnt the "Klear Thoughtz" principle (see my Ebook By Same name **https://sellfy.com/p/kxfC**) you will then fully understand how the routines I have just mentioned both work and amaze audiences on a deeply emotional level.

Incidentally you can then give the person whose exact date of birth has been revealed a Character Reading from the stage which will be confirmed as being amazingly accurate and impressive to them and thus also impress both them and the audience by using my "Lazy Mans Guide To Astrology" which is taught within the pages of my book "Confessions of a Celebrity Psychic" available from all major Magic Dealers.

A final thought on the above ideas is this; take another look at the Fire Signs which we used in this example:

THE FIRE ELEMENT:

ARIES March 21-April 19,

LEO July 23-August 22,

SAGITTARIUS November 22-December 21

If you really wanted to improvise and think on your feet, you could notice who are amongst the Fire Signs at the start of the show and then later in the show point at several apparently random people.

However of course you'd just point at say 5 or 6 people that you recall as being Fire Signs.

You can then have an on stage volunteer tell 5 of the six people at random to sit down leaving only one person stood up in the audience.

I would in this example then say something to them such as:

"Please just think of your star-sign in your minds eye and start to transmit that to me up here on the stage"

"I'm starting to get the impression that your birthday falls during the warmer months, your birthdays not during the summer is it?"

Now the fact is if they are a Leo, they will have been born in either July or August which is the Summer, so will answer YES MY BIRTHDAY IS DURING THE SUMMER, which looks like a miracle to the audience and of course confirms to you they are a Leo because you already know they are a Fire Sign so now you can reveal they are a Leo with perhaps a short Star Sign Reading first leading up to the reveal, or using the "Klear Thoughtz" principle (see ebook of same name) you could have an on stage audience member read their mind and tell them what Star-Sign they are.

If however they say NO MY BIRTHDAY IS NOT IN THE SUMMER, it still looks as though you got this right because of the way you phrased what you said, which although it was a question from your point of view, can be perceived by the audience as being a statement of fact so long as you raise your voice as you say the part in bold of the sentence:

"I'm starting to get the impression that your birthday falls during the warmer months, your birthdays not during the summer is it?"

So if they say NO you can respond by saying something such as:

"Yes that's what I thought, but I sense a warmish time of year, almost as if you have a spring in your step on your birthday would that be correct?"

If they say YES then you know they were born in Spring Time and as such are an Aries born in either March or April, if however they say NO then they must be a Sagittarian born in November or December when it's much colder.

The thing is though as they themselves will have forgotten (as will the audience) that you found out what element everyone's Star Sign was earlier in the show, they will have no idea that you know they are a Fire Sign and as such no idea that you know for a fact that they are either Aries, Leo or Sagittarius.

Therefore the gentle questioning disguised as statements of fact (known as verbal fishing in mentalism) will easily go unnoticed and you can very cleverly find out for certain which of the three fire signs they are without anyone realising you have done this and without anything having ever been written down by anyone at any time.

You can then knowing their Star Sign give them an amazingly accurate character reading which both the audience and them will find hugely impressive prior to either naming their Exact Zodiac Sign yourself or prior to making it look like an onstage volunteer gets it right using the "Klear Thoughtz" gimmick (see ebook of same name) of which you would have 3 gimmicks to hand, namely one for each of the three Fire Signs that they could possibly be.

This of course with some careful thought and wording can be used to walk up to any stranger and ask them to merely think of their Star-Sign and to then write down what element of Star Sign they are.

You can then use a centre tear or any form of Billet peek to find out whether they are Air, Earth, Fire or Water at which point you can use the "verbal fishing" method as just detailed to narrow down which of the 3 possible star signs they are from the element they wrote down in such a manner that you can always in an impressive manner reveal to them their EXACT STAR – SIGN in a manner where they will swear they never wrote it down due to the very real fact that they never did write down their exact Star Sign they only wrote down what element they are.

And given that they have no idea that you managed to peek this information they will truly believe you are Psychic if this approach is used correctly.

And don't forget that at the start of the show you could identify which audience members are married, which are single and which are divorced etc in your opening warm up "Mental Exercises" as you set the scene for the show and this would also give you valuable information about people which can be revealed later in the show in the same manner as just taught here for the Star Signs.

All it takes is just a tiny bit of thought and imagination on your part and using the principles taught in this section along with the Cold-Reading and Verbal Fishing Techniques taught in my book "Confessions of a Celebrity Psychic" and you truly do have some of the most impressive no props required impromptu and stage mentalism available to you that will prove to be reputation making!

As a final thought if you make use of a Thumb Writer (TW) then using the principles I have detailed above you could apparently walk up to a complete stranger, ask them to write the element of their sign onto a slip of paper and fold it up so you can't see it etc..

As they do this you could apparently write a prediction on one of your business cards and place it flat on the table in full view.

Using either the Centre Tear method (CT) or your favourite glimpse you find out what element they are and can then use the Verbal Fishing taught earlier to read their mind and tell them what their element is and also what exact Zodiac Sign they are!

Then as the kicker ending thanks to the use of a Nail Writer such as this one - **http://tinyurl.com/3oswal7** you can ask the volunteer what date of the month they were born on and then are able to show them that this is the number that you had written down on your prediction at the very start of the effect.

If you've really got balls then ask the volunteer 3 questions that you know the answers to and notice where their eyes point when answering these things in a truthful manner.

Once you know this get them to think of which element their star sign is and tell them you will ask them four questions and they are to say NO to them all and try to fool you..

You then ask is their sign Air, Earth, Fire and finally Water. If you watch closely for the three they are telling the truth for when they say No its not right for them their eyes will point where they did for the earlier questions when they told the truth whereas usually when they hit the element which is theirs and are lying by saying NO their eyes will move in a different direction and you'll know by this which element they are.

Once you know that proceed as already explained and with practise you'll have a reputation making effect on your hands.

For the record, although my work on this was not credited in the first few copies sold of "Astro-Divinations" by Paul Voodini and Cashliostro, I am aware that I am now Credited at least twice in the manuscript, as they have now been made aware that I published in my "Klear Thoughtz" ebook years ago the method of discovering what their Element is and then from that using clever wording related to the weather and time of the year in order to work out which of the 3 Signs of that element that actually were born under.

Oh and one final point, you will find that quite a number of people do not seem to know what element their Star Sign is, and even sometimes don't know what their Sign is at all.

These days it is an easy matter to tell them to look it up on the internet as either their own or a friends mobile phone will have internet capability.

Good Luck and Enjoy

Jonathan Royle

(c) Jonathan Royle 2014.

www.magicalguru.com

And for the sake of completeness here is my Lazy Man's Guide to Astrological readings which has been in print for many years in various publications I have put out, taught on various of my DVD packages and most certainly pre-dates for example "Zero to 60" as recently released in 2015 by Michael Murray.

E-Z WAY TO ASTROLOGY

By far the easiest way to learn to do Astrological readings of people is as follows:

1) Write down each of the twelve star signs.

2) Next to these write down to each of the twelve signs the name of a family member or close friend or at worst work colleague who has that particular starsign.

3) Remember which person relates to which starsign and vice versa and then your job of learning basic Astrology is done!

When you are doing readings and find out what the persons starsign is, you quite simply recall which friend or family member you know has that same star sign and then proceed to reel off information about them.

In otherwords as you know your friend or family member inside out, their personality, their bad habits, and their likes/dislikes etc and they have the SAME STARSIGN as the person now sat in front of you, they should therefore have much in common!

I've been using this simple technique for years and have found through personal experience that by describing the character traits, personality, likes/dislikes and bad habits etc of the person you know well with the same sign as your client you will be 99% correct almost 100% of the time!

Obviously you reveal this information to the client sat in front of you as if it is your expertise of Astrology that leads you to say this about them and certainly you do not mention the connection to family/friends!

Learn Astrology this way and you'll be giving simple starsign readings in less than an hour!

ADDITIONAL THOUGHTS & IDEAS

In his manuscript "The Sympathetic Seer", the late Ken De Courcy taught a system for doing readings whereby each letter of the alphabet is given a word that can trigger off things to say to the person you are doing the reading for.

You then find out their name and use each letter of their name in turn to use the word listed in the system to set you off saying things to the person and this is repeated for each letter of their name.

I have used (and taught) essentially that idea but without learning any list of words for many, many years now.

I find out the persons first and last name and then go through letter by letter from the start of their name to as far as I need to in order to kill the amount of time needed in the particular circumstances.

I take the letter and use it to think of the first descriptive word that I can think of that starts with that letter, and then I conjure up a sentence containing that descriptive word and state it to the person having the reading as one of my Psychic Vibrations about them.

As long as I keep getting positive responses I keep on saying the first thing that comes into my head which is triggered off by the thing I just said to them and keep doing such until I get a negative response, at which time I proceed to the next letter of their name and start the process again.

From what I understand Michael Murray in his 2015 Release "Zero to 90" has essentially taken the idea and concept that I have explained as my easy way to Astrology in so much as talking about people you know already and stating that information to the person sat in front of you and has combined it with taking each letter of the persons name and using that as a trigger for a process of "Free Association" to trigger off ideas in your mind.

In Michael's case I understand that he advises that for each letter of the person you are doing the reading for, you take that letter of their name and think of the first person you know personally (or know of/about) whose name starts with that same letter and then you tell the person sat in front of you all about that persons life, personality, challenges etc.

You continue doing so as long as you are getting "hits" and when you get a negative response you move onto the next letter of their name and do the same thing.

Given the vast number of years that my "Easy Astrology" method has been in print and also the years my version of the A to Z System has been taught on DVD and in print etc, combined with the information published sometimes decades ago by the likes of Kenton Knepper, I can most certainly say that there is nothing that could really be considered new in "Zero to 90" by Michael Murray.

COLD-READING COMBINED WITH THE CENTRE TEAR

Watch this video which is extracted from the massive Home Study Video Course "Confessions of a Hypnotist" which is available to buy from this link: **https://sellfy.com/p/oQjK/**from the starting point of One Hour and

19 Minutes **https://youtu.be/kAKdBQ7Kr8U?t=1h19m**

In that video, which for the record is now over ten years old, you will see a short video of me combining Cold Reading with the fact that I have obtained the name of someone in Spirit by using the "Centre Tear" technique.

Although only a short demonstration I hope that it gives you an idea of just how powerful these incredibly simple techniques can be when presented with conviction and the attitude that suggests what you are doing is genuine!

Incidentally if you were to purchase that video set, then you will find that there is some excellent advice and training on using Pendulums for Psychic Entertainment and also for therapeutic purposes taught in the set, along with a whole bunch of other very powerful Mentalism and Psychic Style Entertainment Stuff as well, which I am sure you would be able to Make great use of.

That link again to secure your copy is: **https://sellfy.com/p/oQjK/**

There are of course a whole host of different impression pads, clipboards and even electronic devices now on the market which could also be used pre-show, ideally by a staff member who asks a few people to write down the names of loved ones, then to take the piece of paper they have written the name on and fold it up and place it into their pocket so it is "close" to them and thus will help them to attract the person from Spirit and make the chances of Spirit Communication all that more likely when the platform demonstration begins later that night.

An impression (copy) of what they wrote is of course obtained by the device and your staff member takes note of where the person/s are sitting so that this can be noted down and passed onto you before the show begins.

I kept things really simple and used carbon paper stuck into a normal writing pad a few pages down.

Very low tech, cheap and easy to make and always worked well to get an impression of what they had written on the sheet of paper which was a few pages above where the Carbon Paper was stuck in place.

Half a dozen of these pads is more than enough to get information from 6 different people before the show begins and that is more than enough to give 3 Mega Accurate pieces of information in the first half of the show and another 3 pieces in the second half of the show which will blow them away.

I can also reveal that we also used an electronic device called "The Whisper 2000" which you can see images, video and information about on Google at this link: **http://tinyurl.com/pxkfdar**

Using this device it was possible to listen in on the conversations of audience members both before the show began and also during the interval and by so doing it was always easy to obtain information that could be used in the show, as more often than not they would be talking about deceased friends and relatives of whom they desired to get some form of contact and message from by attending that night.

Armed with such information it was easy to throw these bits of information out as "I'm being told by Spirit to say XYZ" (XYZ being the information you obtained) "Does that make any sense or connection for anybody here tonight?"

Obviously the person/s whom you overheard speaking about these things will indicate that it means something to them and you can then feed them more of what you overheard as if it is coming from "Spirit"

Another ploy that we used with great effect was to give Free Tickets to our stage demonstrations to people who had come to us for personal one to one readings.

This guaranteed that we had several people in our audiences whom we already knew tons about and prior to the show could also have spent a little bit of time to do some further research on them, thus enabling us to get very accurate information from "Spirit" to reveal to them during the show.

We would also research the Obituary's as printed in the Local Papers that were on sale in a 10 mile radius of the venue where we were performing and on occasion would even visit the local grave yards to get information from headstones.

These names of recently deceased (those who passed within a few weeks before the date of our shows) and also the names of those who passed around a year ago (give or take a few weeks each way) from the date of our show were noted and were thrown out to the audience as names we were getting contact with from the other side.

The chances were that as the person had passed recently or due to the fact it was very close to the anniversary of them passing, this increased the chances of a family member of friend of that person being present in the room.

These days such advance research can so much more easily be done at home by way of using the internet to access newspaper archives and local birth and death records and such like.

Also on the internet if you search for things such as "Statistics Death in UK" or replace UK with the area you will be performing and you can get much information that can prove of use.

Indeed search a little and there are websites galore that will tell you what the most popular names for babies being born this year are, what the most popular names were for men and women in certain years, what the most likely causes of death were, the most likely professions and such like.

In other words the internet has made it even easier than ever to gain advance information and use what is known as "Hot Reading" in your shows.

Consider this, if you sell advance tickets to your event through a site such as **www.eventbrite.com** then you will end up with the name and email address of the person who is booking the tickets, and if they pay using paypal you will also have their postal address as well.

Using Google it is now an easy matter to search their name, email and postal address to find out tons about them.

Often you will be able to find their Facebook, Linkedin, Twitter and other Social Media Accounts thanks to their name and email address.

Using their address you can use Google Maps and Street View to actually look at the exterior of their house and their street which gives you even more amazingly accurate information to feed to them as part of your reading as if you are being told it by their loved ones in Spirit.

Use your initiative and for example from their name, address and email you can end up seeing their Social Media Accounts and then know what they look like from some photographs, also this will more often than not reveal links to their family members and friends and what they look like.

A quick look at some of the groups they have joined on Social Media reveals to you their interests and hobbies, and well I hope you are getting the idea.

One piece of information can lead to revealing something else like a mention on their social media of where they work, which then means you can research that company and well by now I trust you get the idea.

With Spiritualist shows it is always wise (where possible) to sell tickets on the basis that seats are allocated on the night by virtue of who arrives there and claims their seats first.

Generally speaking those people who show up first and get seated in the first few rows will be major believers and of such a mind state that they will practically agree to most anything and everything you say to them.

Which reminds me of another trick we used to use before big shows, namely that of attending a service at the Spiritualist Churches local to the venue where the show is taking place.

We would give them a poster to display at the venue which ensured plenty of sales as those who attend these places are often serial Psychic and Clairvoyant show attendees.

But whilst there we would sit in on the service with a hidden pocket tape recorder which would be recording everything.

After leaving we would then be able to take notes from the tape giving details about those who were there and got messages and knowing that even if that person themselves did not attend the show, at least a few members of the Church who knew them would and thus when you gave out this information about them apparently from Spirit, there would most likely be someone in the room who it would ring a bell with and would readily accept the message and pass it onto their friend later as we would of course request them to.

Remember that if you ever feel like you are running out of things to say, you can just ask them what their name and star sign is and then use my Easy Astrology System and also letters of the Alphabet System to give you more than enough to keep you talking and getting a good number of hits.

I really would advise you to go and see as many different live Clairvoyants as Possible doing demonstrations both in theatres and also those in Church type environments as you will without doubt learn more from observing these people at work than you ever will from any book or DVD.

Indeed in truth you will learn far more by actually just getting out there and doing it, such is many peoples need to believe, that they will often accept most anything you say as reality.

And from personal experience of over 25+ years to date of both doing Stage "Contacting the Dead" shows and also one to one Tarot and Psychic Readings (which I continued to do and have done for the past 25+ years even when I stopped the contacting the dead shows) I can tell you without any hesitations that the people who come to these shows in the main just want to get some kind of message and answers to the problems on their minds.

They are not bothered in the slightest how you find out what their questions are, they truly are only interested in the answers.

And thus as Paul Voodini has mentioned in one of his brilliant publications entitled "Pure Q and A" you can quite literally have bits of card on everybodys chairs with pencils/pens and have everybody told as they arrive by your front of house staff that they should put their seat number, name and a question they would like to have answered by Spirit onto the card and then drop it into the large bowl at the front of the stage.

You could then quite literally in full view of everybody just select a card from the large clear plastic container, quickly read what is on it and then discard it in your pocket.

At this point you can start to "sense" things coming through from the other side and then can go to the right person as their seat number was on the card along with their name and a question they want answering by Spirit.

The information that was on the card combined with the clues you will get from the way the person is dressed, how old they look and such will all give you more than enough of an idea what to say and talk about.

It's all very much a matter of common sense and giving sensible advice to them and believe me, if you use this cards technique during the first half of the show and then come interval time, have a member of your staff remove the bowl from the stage and bring it to you in your dressing room, by the end of the show most will forget that the bowl was ever there or that you ever went near it and/or got information from what they had written down.

And of course during the interval you can commit to memory the details from about half a dozen of the cards, or if your really lazy, write the key points large onto a massive Flip Chart Pad which on its stand can be located in the wings of the theatre (side of the stage) so that although the audience cannot see it, you can easily glance at it and be reminded of the secrets it contains as you wander about the stage apparently talking to people from the Spirit World.

Another thing to bear in mind is that giving such a show is essentially just giving a number of one to one readings to different people one after the other whilst everybody else watches and listens.

In other words all of the techniques described in this manuscript for use in giving personal one to one readings can also be used within the context of a Platform Clairvoyance and Psychic demonstration.

Heck I have even seen people, with great success, stand on stage and take out a deck of Tarot Cards, get the chosen audience member to select 3 of them and then the performer has given a simple 3 Card Tarot Reading from the stage as the main time filler of what they were doing and then they just occasionally made out that they were getting a message from Spirit.

TAROT CARDS – THE RIDER WAITE DECK

When you have listened to the Audio Lesson on how to remember the meanings of the Tarot Cards to which a link is given earlier in this manuscript, then the details that follow will serve as additional memory joggers for you.

THE TEN NUMBER'S

01 = Starts & Beginnings of Journey (one is the first number)

02 = Partnerships (Two is a pair – a couple)

03 = Difficulties (two's company threes a crowd)

04) = Foundations for the Future (four corners of house)

05) = Difficult until learn the secret (drawing a five pointed star)

06) = Success & Luck (throwing a Six on Dice)

07) = Lesson's To Be Learnt (play games at school till age 7)

08) = Going Round In Circles (draw number eight and end up at start)

09) = Almost There (only one more number to go or one more step on journey)

10) = Final Destination & Success (End of journey is a result)

THE FOUR COURT – PICTURE CARDS

PAGE = Younger Female Figure

KNIGHT = Younger Male Figure

QUEEN = Older Female Figure

KING = Older Male Figure

THE FOUR SUIT'S OF THE TAROT DECK

CUPS = Loving Cups = Relationship Matter's

WANDS or STAFFS = Fire of my life = Social Interactions/environment

COINS or PENTACLES = Money & Material Matters

SWORD'S = Two Sides Sharp & Dull – Communications

THE PLAYING CARD'S FOUR SUIT'S

HEART'S = Cups (hearts = Relationships)

CLUB'S = Wands (it's a club or staff type stick)

DIAMOND'S = Coins (diamonds are worth money)

SPADE'S = Swords (are pointed at top like a sword)

THE PLAYING CARD PICTURE CARD'S

JACK = Page & Knight (So younger male & female figures)

QUEEN = Queen = Older Female Figure

KING = King = Older Male Figure

THE PLAYING CARD NUMBER CARD'S

The numbers on cards (1 to 10) relate in same way to the numbers 1 to 10 do for Tarot Cards as explained earlier.

THE TAROT CARDS SET & PLAYING CARD'S

*There are 78 Cards in total in a trot deck (52 in playing cards)

*There are four suits in both decks of cards and tarot.

*Tarot has 14 cards in each suit (playing Cards have 13 cards each suit)

*The Tarot has 56 number & court cards (playing cards have 52) in tarot these are known as the Minor Arcana cards.

*The Tarot also has 22 other cards (makes 78 total) known as The Major Arcana cards.

THE DECK OF (PLAYING CARD'S) LYRIC'S

During the North African Campaign, a bunch of soldier boys had been on a long hike. They arrived in a little town called Casino. The next morning being Sunday, several of the boys went to church. A sergeant commanded the boys in church.

After the Chaplain read the prayer, the text was taken up next. Those of the boys that had a prayer book took them out. One boy had only a deck of cards, and he spread them out. The sergeant saw the cards and said, "Soldier, put away those cards." After the service was over, the soldier was taken prisoner and brought before the Provost Marshal.

The Marshal said, "Sergeant, why have you brought this man here?"

"For playing cards in church, Sir," was the response.

The Marshal asked the soldier, "And what have you to say for yourself, son?"

"Much, Sir," replied the soldier.

The Marshal stated, "I hope so, for if not I will punish you more than any man was ever punished."

The soldier said, "Sir, I have been on the march for about six months. I have neither bible nor a prayer book, but I hope to satisfy you, sir, with the purity of my intentions." And with that, the boy started his story ...

"You see, sir, when I look at the Ace, it reminds me that there is but one God."

And the deuce reminds me that the bible is divided into two parts: the Old and the New Testaments.

When I see the trey, I think of the Father, the Son, and the Holy Spirit. And when I see the four, I think of the four evangelists who preached the Gospel: there was Matthew, Mark, Luke and John.

And when I see the five, it reminds me of the five wise virgins who trimmed their lamps; there were ten of them: five were wise and were saved, five were foolish and were shut out.

When I see the six, it reminds me that in six days God made this heaven and earth.

And when I see the seven, it reminds me that on the seventh day, God rested from his great work.

And when I see the eight, I think of the eight righteous persons that God saved when he destroyed the earth: there was Noah, his wife, their sons and their wives.

And when I see the nine, I think of the lepers our saviour cleansed, and that nine of the ten didn't even thank him.

When I see the ten, I think of the ten commandments that God handed down to Moses on a tablet of stone.

When I see the King, it reminds me that there is but one King of Heaven, God Almighty.

And when I see the Queen, I think of the blessed Virgin Mary who is the Queen of Heaven.

And the Jack or Knave is the Devil.

When I count the number of spots in a deck of cards, I find 365, the number of days in a year.

There are 52 cards, the number of weeks in a year.

There are four suits, the number of weeks in a month.

There are twelve picture cards, the number of months in a year.

There are thirteen tricks, the number of weeks in a quarter.

So you see, Sir, my deck of cards serves me as a bible, an almanac and a prayer book."

The author and performer of "Deck of Cards" was
T. Texas Tyler.
He stated at the conclusion:
"And friends, this story is true.
I know ... I was that soldier."

THE MAJOR ARCANA – THE 22 FUNNY PICTURE CARD'S

00 = THE FOOL = Foolish decisions – Joker – Idiot – Daft & Crazy

01 = THE MAGICIAN = Paul Daniel's – David Blaine – devious – skilful – deceit – hiding stuff in front of your eyes.

02 = HIGH PRIESTESS = Female religious Symbol – good influence & balance – think of like a female Pope giving good advice.

03 = EMPRESS = You Know someone – an older wise woman.

04 = EMPEROR = You Know someone an older wise man.

05 = HIEROPHANT or POPE = Religious Preacher - wise – good advice.

06 = LOVER'S = Look Happy – harmony – love.

07 = CHARIOT = to win the chariot race is hard but rewards are good – overcoming obstacles and struggles in path of life.

08 = STRENGTH = Inner Strength to carry on.

09) = THE HERMIT = Sad – lonely – hidden away – on own.

10) = WHEEL OF FORTUNE = game show & winning prizes – its lucky.

11) = JUSTICE = scales of justice will balance out – legal?

12) = HANGED MAN = confused – restricted – blood to head – dizzy.

13) = DEATH = End of the old and start of the new. Changes for future.

14) = TEMPERANCE = Moderation in all things required.

15) = DEVIL = Lived backwards – thing or person not what they seem – control.

16) = THE TOWER = No doors – hard to enter – difficulties.

17) = THE STAR = wish upon a lucky star and dreams can come true.

18) = MOON = werewolf gets moody at moon – changes – split personality.

19) = SUN = makes things grow – light – healing & growth.

20) = JUDGEMENT = Piggy in the middle – others judging you?

21) = WORLD = worlds a wonderful place – make best of it etc.

NOTE: As the FOOL is regarded as card Zero that is the total 22 Cards of The Major Arcana.

SECRETS OF PAST LIFE REGRESSIONS

Another style of performance that the "Spiritualist" and "Shut Eye" market love are "Evenings of Past Life Regression" for which you can see above the poster I use to promote such events.

Should you desire to present events such as these, then it truly is really as simple as learning How to Safely Hypnotize people which I teach in depth on "The Transparency Template" DVDs as per: **https://sellfy.com/p/3JIZ/**

Then basically if you copy what I do in the two example videos that follow you should basically get similar results.

Part One: **https://youtu.be/Rbvo9se4FrE**

Part Two: **https://youtu.be/-w2zbQFgC60**

Once they are "under" Hypnosis I am basically suggesting to them that they are in a library which has lots of shelves and book cases in it which are stacked from ceiling to floor with numerous different types of books.

Big books and small books, Paperback and Hardback, New Books and Really old Antique books with fancy covers and gold leaf embossed writing on their spine and indeed every other type of book you could ever possibly imagine.

They are told that on the count of three, that in their minds eye they are going to imagine, that it is "almost as if" they will instantly reach up towards one of the shelves and will instantly be drawn towards one book which feels right for them which they will then pull off the shelve.

This is done and then they are told that this time on the count of three that they will open the book randomly to a page and on that page they will discover a picture of a time in the past which they will be able to imagine themselves jumping into and taking a look around.

Once they are "inside" the picture the process of asking them open ended questions so as to encourage them to say things is begun as you can see on the videos.

Basically that is all there is to it, although sometimes I might suggest that in a moment I will count to 3 and then you'll instantly be back out of the picture in that book and will replace the book onto the shelve and pick another one instead.

As simplistic as that may sound, that is all there is to it really once you have got them Hypnotized, which as I have already said you would be wise to learn how to do Properly and Safely by studying "The Transparency Template" DVD Set which is available here: **https://sellfy.com/p/3JIZ/**

I would also advise engaging the Services of a Psychic Artist who you ask to draw pictures of what they feel the people looked like when they were in their past lives.

As you can see in the videos this adds a whole extra level to things and can, as seen in the videos, make the whole thing seem even more amazing.

In terms of recommended reading on the subject of Past Life Regressions, the best book I have ever read on the subject and the one which got me started earning good money giving one to one Past Life Regression Sessions well over two decades ago is "Cashing In On Past Lifes" by Richard Webster.

<u>SOME FINAL THOUGHTS</u>

Before I bring this short publication to an end, I would just like to say that in regards to running events such as those advertised in the above poster, you would be wise to check out the works of Paul Voodini which can be found on his site of: **http://www.readerofminds.co.uk/**

But I will say this, having worked with Paul Voodini on several occasions and also having used what he teaches in his excellent books on the Art of Seances, I can honestly state that when the lights are turned off and the room plunges into darkness whilst people are all stood in a circle holding hands and told to breathe deeply and regularly in through their nose and then out through their mouths, it does not take long at all before people start to claim to have heard things or to have felt or "sensed" things.

The imagination is a very powerful thing and when someone is stood in a dark room in a place they don't know, which has usually been advertised as being "Haunted" then it does not take long for most peoples minds to run riot.

Regarding Ouija Boards and Pendulums, I talk about these and teach the use of Pendulums in the "Confessions of a Hypnotist" video set available here: **https://sellfy.com/p/oQjK/**

However in brief the main Secret is that they both work by Ideo Motor Response which basically means that the person is making the Pendulum move by moving it themselves but it is their unconscious mind that is making this happen and so often even they are amazed.

The same applies to Ouija Boards as well, a good understanding of Stage Hypnosis Techniques and Suggestion and your ability to use Pendulums and Ouija Boards effectively in your work will be vastly improved and in that regards you would be wise to obtain a copy of "The Transparency Template" DVDS from: **https://sellfy.com/p/3JIZ/**

Your money would be well spent booking a place and attending at the next Ghost Hunt and Psychic Experiments type night that is taking place in your area.

Attend, Participate, Pay attention to everything and REMEMBER what the host/presenter says and does and what occurs during the night.

Generally speaking do as they do and say as they say and to a greater of lesser extent you will get the same kind of results, indeed often better when you have an understanding of Stage Hypnosis and Suggestion

Techniques which many of these "Shut Eyes" don't have a clue about.

In terms of giving accurate readings both one to one and also from the Stage, my final piece of advice would be to Study the Art of Body Language as understanding such can tell you tons about the person you are doing the reading for.

Also in terms of a Stage Demonstration, once you have found out who the person you are doing the reading for is sat with (how many people, whom etc) then you can also observe their body language which will give you tons of clues as you give out your information from "Spirit" to the person they all know.

And when it comes to Body Language I unreservedly recommend this set of training DVDS by British Television & Media Body Language Expert Robert Phipps - **https://sellfy.com/p/WDfg/**

To bring this book to a close I am going to give you a few website links to take a look at that each contain much valuable Free Information, which when studied with the contents of this book in mind will reveal much of worth to you.

www.skeptic.com/downloads/10_Easy_Psychic_Lessons.pdf

http://en.wikipedia.org/wiki/Cold_reading

http://www.psychicscience.org/coldread.aspx

http://teacherluke.co.uk/2012/10/11/117-psychics-cold-reading-barnum-statements/

http://www.straightdope.com/columns/read/2132/how-come-tv-psychics-seem-so-convincing

http://en.wikipedia.org/wiki/Mediumship

http://en.wikipedia.org/wiki/Spiritualism

https://www.psychologytoday.com/blog/speaking-in-tongues/201201/tricks-the-psychic-trade

http://www.libertymagazine.com/icons_houdini.htm

http://www.badpsychics.com/

Remember that as human being's we are all basically the same, hence the fact that the mnemonic coined by Herb Dewey (King of the Cold Readers) stating that the Secret to Powerful Psychic Readings was:

THE SCAM

This being an aid to remember that the components and elements that you need to include in a reading are subjects and information covering:

Travel - Health – Education

Sex - Career - Ambitions - Money

Cover all of those areas and you are **GUARANTEED** Success.

Good Luck and Thank You For Purchasing This Book.

Many Thanks

Jonathan Royle

PS: Please be Sure to check out the Shop on my website at where you will find many items of great interest to Magician's, Mentalist's, Hypnotists and Psychic Entertainers - **www.magicalguru.com**

PPS: By way of saying Thanks for buying this Ebook, I would like to offer you a Massive 50% Discount off my "Elite Hypnosis Bootcamp and Passive Hypnosis Profits" 2.0 Platinum Edition. Just enter the Voucher code **LAUNCH** (in block capitals) where it asks for the voucher code and you will SAVE 50% off the usual price of this amazing package at:

http://www.yescourse.com/store/elite-hypnosis-bootcamp-passive-hypnosis-profits-platinum-edition-20/

STOP-PRESS – STOP PRESS – STOP PRESS – STOP PRESS

I was not intending to share this final technique with you, a technique that has enabled me to "Cure" people of their issues on Stage and also in one to one therapy sessions with success and in a matter of just a few minutes, but heck, in for a penny in for a pound.

When I use this in "Serious Psychic Shows" I tell them they are tapping their Psychic Third Eye (Centre of Forehead), Their Base Chakra (Just below the Navel) and then are also tapping on their Left and Right upper areas of their bodies as this signify's balance and harmony.

That should all make sense once you have watched this Short Video teaching my "Complete Mind Tapping" technique:

REVIEW FROM JON SCOTLAND

This is a really interesting read for both skeptics and believers alike

This is a book by a guy who has actually " Been there done that " and comes from experience and not just research.

I have been fortunate to meet Alex on a number of occasions and he certainly has a wealth of knowledge in his field.

There is some really powerful material here , use it as you will but please think of others and their feelings when you do

A MUST READ FOR THOSE WITH AN INTEREST IN THE PSYCHIC WORLD REGARDLESS OF BELIEFS

Jon Scotland
www.psychicexperiments.co.uk

REVIEW FROM RAY RONSON

Having purchased products from Alex in the past and performed impromptu many of the mentalism material learned after my own hypnotism show I was looking forward to reviewing this latest publication as i've never felt disappointed with any of Alex's (Jonathon's) products i've viewed.

Firstly I would like to point out that some of the methods revealed, in my opinion are genius in their simplicity to learn and with practised patter may turn you into a what others consider a psychic or medium superstar!

I tend to lean toward readings rather than the medium/contacting the dead angle and their is plenty of material here to get stuck into, especially as this latest publication also has links to video instruction which is a treasure trove in itself.

The section on astrology is a gem, well explained and so simple to put into play as the system works on easy mnemonics. Included is a system to guide you through any style of reading you prefer, ive used this system as a framework for my readings for years now and once again with a little practise of impromptu patter this system is dynamite, used along with the astrological system this will make your readings awsome.

If you are just starting your journey in the world of psychic entertainment or even an experienced entertainer wanting to make a cross over into another form of entertainment this book is a must!

Ray Ronson – Hypnotist and actor (IMDB Ray Ronson)
http://www.stage-hypnotist.net/

REVIEW FROM RICK KIRKBY

Having read – The Psychic Secrets Of Alex-Leroy, and being part of the Paranormal scene since I was 15, I can honestly say, I have witnessed first-hand many of the techniques, used in this pdf- that have both fooled me in the past and many others alike, so called paranormal experts too....

You see although what is taught, may seem simple (it pretty much is) the way peoples minds work, this is what creates the phenomenon, the reaction the hits!!!

Just as with magic, some of the best effects happen, within the person's own mind!!

This is a great stepping stone into the world of psychic entertainment, but hopefully on the grounds of just that entertainment.. But hey ho I'm not your farther lol… So to sum it all up… This is yet another great book by Alex, and one that you will refer to time and time again!!

Rick Kirkby C.Ht.
IMdb Accredited Producer for Art Of The Ghost Hunter.
And Paranormal Investigator and Paranormal Consultant.

REVIEW BY WAYNE DHARANA

As always Alex aka Jonathan Royle is overdelivering, and revealing the REAL secrets of the entertainment world.

In this instance opening up completely about the world of psychic entertainment.

This Book is a COMPLETE course on all things psychic, and is clearly the result of many years working as both a psychic performer, hypnotist, mentalist, and all round performer.

Not only are you getting the REAL secrets of how to conduct a full legth psychic/ mediumship show… but you even get the details that would allow you to work full time offering tarot readings, psychic counselling etc.

Not to mention the tips and advice about how to actually get the work through the publicity tips and advice on standing out from the crowd.

The kind of tips that only come from tried and tested routines and real world experience.

I would whole heartedly reccomend this to anyone interested in either propless mentalism, psychic entertainment, or indeed anyone simply wanting to create more 'imapct' with thier existing performances, through connecting and resonating with people on a very real, but 'energetic' level."

Wayne Dharana
www.lifeconfidencewarrior.com

Review in nine sentences of:
THE PSYCHIC SECRETS OF ALEX-LEROY By: JONATHAN ROYLE

Disclaimer#1: Been Favored with a Review Copy.

Disclaimer#2: Feeling quite overwhelmed now due to the detailed and eye opening Techniques provided. Their smooth Description blew out quite a Firework of the associated Ideas in my Mind!

The Author, the one and only, the amazing Alex-LeRoy is sharing an astonishingly direct to the point and easy to understand and put to immediate use bundle of tested recipes in effecting and duplicating all the major feats of the famous name psychics whom are "apparently" not just in the business of performing clever tricks.

This Book is neither for timid minds, nor a noob!

Fairly Endorsed for an average self- responsible Amateur as well as an experienced Speaker and even World Class Psychic Performers will no doubt learn a thing or two.

A very comprehensive collection of techniques to ensure your success.

Appreciatively, Holistic Zen Baltilund, aka Your Bottom Line Therapist.
The Netherlands, 25th April, 2015

REVIEW BY CHRIS BYNG

Whether you want to introduce a psychic element to your magic, confidently work the Psychic Fayre circuit or put on a full evening of psychic entertainment, this is the PDF you will need.

It comprehensively covers all the bases.

Here we discover the mechanics of numerous effects and routines with performance notes and, very importantly, explanations of the psychology behind the performance.

Even the choice of background music is covered.

Do not miss this one.

Chris Byng – Professional Tarot Reader and Psychic Entertainer.
http://luciferstemple.com/

REVIEW BY BRIAN STRACNER

This is one of those rare priceless books which not only teaches valuable effects, but it also outlines a whole professional psychic show from Alex's own personal repertoire.

This is not only valuable for someone who wants to learn how to work as a professional psychic, but it is also a fantastic example of how a working psychic structures a show.

As a working pro myself, I can personally attest to the value contained within this wonderful book.

~Brian (HypnoSwami) Stracner~
http://www.funhypnosisshow.com/

REVIEW BY CHRIS DAVIES

Review of 'The Psychic Secrets of Alex Leroy'

Ok so I have just got through reading a copy of this latest piece by Alex Leroy aka Jonathan Royle.

He covers a lot of ground in this work, not all of it is to my taste and Jonathan himself acknowledges that there are potential moral challenges faced when presenting some of this material.

The argument for sharing the how's and the why's of how some of these 'miracles' occur is that by sharing this knowledge it will/can open people's eyes to the scam artists that operate and prey on the vulnerable.

It would indeed be possible for someone to learn this material and to present a show that served to debunk the would-be scammers.

Some of the material I have been familiar with through other sources, most of which Jonathan claims to pre-date (I use the word 'claims' simply because I do not possess the knowledge of publication dates to validate nor dismiss the claim), either way it is useful to hear it from another source and in a slightly different way as it gives more food for thought and presentation ideas.

There is one piece in particular in which I disagreed with the information presented. The piece referred to the base chakra as being aligned with the navel. The base chakra (mooladhara) is aligned with the ovaries and gonads, I believe the chakra that he is referring to is the sacral chakra (svadisthana), although this sits below the navel area in the sacral region this would then make more sense with his colour choice of orange – red relates to the base chakra, orange to the sacral chakra and yellow to the navel chakra (manipura; at the solar plexus or navel).

Now it may seem that I am splitting hairs here, especially when considered against the knowledge that it is all trickery, 'smoke and mirrors', persuasion etc. However, I am a Yoga instructor amongst other things so this information if presented as part of an act would have destroyed the performers credibility in my eyes. Whilst we as the performers know it to be trickery, we want our audiences to believe and, importantly, they want to believe. Given the number of people who practice Yoga nowadays and the amount of information readily available on the Chakras, it would make sense to get this level of detail right prior to presenting it if you want to keep your audience 'on-side'.

As I said earlier, Jonathan covers a lot of ground in this work so it's not surprising that not all of it resonates with me, there is sufficient information contained within to make its reading a worthwhile endeavour and the techniques he shares are simple and they have been tried and tested over time.

If you have an interest in Psychic entertaining then the information contained within this work will be of use to you and the links provided to further external reading/viewing (some free, some not) will also serve to further your career and potential earnings.

It is, in summary, a generous offering from Jonathan and I have no doubt that anyone will be pleased with their purchase of it.

Chris Davis Dip.C.Hyp/NLP
Hypnotist, MIND Coach & Psychic dabbler.
https://uk.linkedin.com/in/mapcoaching

PUBLISHERS NOTE: Evidence That I Both Used and also Published these techniques (the ones Chris is unsure about) before the recent day "Famous Names" is easily supplied by virtue of the fact that Club 71 published many of them in 1996 and 1997 as submitted to them by me in 1995 and The Supreme Magic Company's Magicgram Magazine published
others back in Circa 1993/1994 time. Also various respectable people who can easily be checked with (should anyone desire) are quoted as confirming that they have seen the evidence and proof that International Newspapers featured me performing these things as far back as 1990/1991 times.

REVIEW BY HARRIZON THE HYPNOTIST

Royle's thoughts on Psychic Entertainment are invaluable to anyone looking at improving or expanding an existing act, or starting in the business.

There is a lot of psychology based on real world experience over a number of years, within these pages, sure to be of use to open eye mediums, fortune tellers and even magicians and mentalists who might not want to associate themselves with presenting true psychic powers.

I've used many of the techniques, ploys and methods described, as taught to me by Jonathan, over the last few years, and have had some amazing reactions!

S. Cassells aka Harrizon The Hypnotist
http://www.harrizon.com/

(**NOTE** – for reasons which I hope are obvious, I've missed-spelt my real last name, and not included a web-address for that side of the business… I don't want this review falling into the hands of future clients!)

REVIEW BY GRAHAM KEMPSTER

This is many books in one, covering psychic skills, cold reading and tarot reading to name just a few.

Full of links (some secret) to YouTube videos, ebook and more….. Also references to books that will help skyrocket your succes in these areas.

Jonathan/ Alex took 26 years to learn his trade, you can really tell the techniques being taught have been honed in the real world.

The Uri Gellar explanations I found fascinating. I honestly Can't recommend this enough.

It is easily worth 10 times the tiny price being asked.

THE END.

Graham Kempster.

REVIEW BY MAX KAAN

Britain has indeed got talent and it need look no further Than Jonathan Royle,

He is in my opinion a must read Author. And in his latest book "The Psychic Secrets of Alex-Leroy" he reveals all of his, until now, most jealously guarded secrets for "Psychic Success" Unreservedly reccomended.

MAX KAAN – Master Hypnotist & Mind Expert
http://www.maxkaan.com/

Review by John Machniak

"If you're a lay person and want to know how 'psychics' perform some of their 'miracles,' this book is something that you'll want to read. If you're a mentalist, magician and published author like me (for over 40 years!!) and never tire of learning, you'll want to read this book, too.

"The best 'take-away' from this book is the author's clear understanding and explanation of the 'power of suggestion' and how this power can help to explain so many 'miracles' that so many people desperately want to believe in. It's as keen a book on the 'nuts and bolts' psychology of human nature as it is an expose of some of the techniques and methods used by some 'psychics.'

"I found especially interesting the author's expose on using modern day technology to gather information for 'psychic messages' and other 'miracles.' (Houdini meets Zuckerberg?)

"The author touches on hypnotism, as well, and any hypnotist or psychotherapist would, I think, find pages 39-40 to be most informative. I'm a certified professional and consulting hypnotist and a master's in counseling student, and I think that the theories offered on these two pages on why 'change' happens, whether in a hypnotic or therapy session, are pretty 'spot on' and well worth knowing.

"Lastly, the author gives some web links to his own products as well as a few informative websites — which cost the reader nothing to search — for anyone interested in learning more about how 'psychics' perform their seeming 'miracles.'

"Anyone who wants to learn a little bit more about how the human mind creates the illusion of what it wants to believe will find some of the answers in this book."

Anyone who wants to contact me can do so at johnmachniak@gmail.com or "John Philip Machniak" on Facebook. I'm always interested in connecting with others who share my interests.

Review by John Machniak

Printed in Great Britain
by Amazon